EVERYTHING
YOU EVER WANTED
TO KNOW ABOUT

(BUT WERE TOO AFRAID TO ASK)

Everything You Ever Wanted to Know About Rugby But Were too Afraid to Ask
ISBN: 9781408114940

Everything You Ever Wanted to Know About Cricket But Were too Afraid to Ask
ISBN: 9781408114957

Everything You Ever Wanted to Know About Golf But Were too Afraid to Ask
ISBN: 9781408114971

Note

Whilst every effort has been made to ensure that the content of this book
is as technically accurate and as sound as possible, neither the author nor the
publishers can accept responsibility for any injury or loss sustained as a result
of the use of this material.

Published by A&C Black Publishers Ltd
36 Soho Square, London W1D 3QY
www.acblack.com

Copyright © 2010 Iain Macintosh

ISBN 978 1 4081 1496 4

Acknowledgements
Cover photographs © shutterstock.com
Illustrations by kja-artists
Designed by James Watson

This book is produced using paper that is made from wood grown in managed,
sustainable forests. It is natural, renewable and recyclable. The logging and
manufacturing processes conform to the environmental regulations of the
country of origin.

Typeset in Giovanni Book by seagulls.net, London

Printed and bound in Berkshire, England by Cox & Wyman

Contents

Acknowledgements

This book is dedicated to my parents, particularly my mum whose involvement in the proofreading stages turned her from the kind of person who thought Glenn Hoddle was a single malt whiskey to someone who can concisely explain the advantages of a high defensive line. It was all a bit unnerving, to be honest with you.

My wonderful wife Rachael wasn't actually my wife when I wrote this and it's a wonder that she actually went through with the wedding ceremony after all that she had to put up with in 2009. Her love sustained me throughout this process and I am a very lucky chap indeed to have had her by my side.

My publisher Charlotte Atyeo was brave enough to hand this project to me and for that she has my eternal thanks. Her colleague Lucy Beevor was brave enough to spell-check and edit the original drafts and for that she has my eternal sympathy.

As always, the online community of Shrimperzone.com, the world's most popular unofficial Southend United website, were on hand to help me out with a few things. Thanks go to Matt the Shrimp, Napster, Firestorm, Dave, Rusty Shackleford, A Century United, Choggy, BluesrBest, LondonBlue, Uxbridge, RaleighWeir, Supablues, Hove Shrimper, Canvey Shrimper, McNasty and Shrimpero. Those are their real names, by the way.

Thanks also to Tony Pearson, Toby Fuhrman, Tom Warren, Shaun Nickless, Dan Bourke, James Findlay, Matt Gallagher, Dave Adams, Phil Adams, Mikey Grady and everyone at The Endeavour Pub in Chelmsford.

Oh, and Joseph Tate? This is for you when you're old enough.

Thanks, finally, to Steve Brierley and his eagle eyes in the late proofreading stages.

Author's note

As this book is written with the primary aim of telling people how mind-bogglingly wonderful football is without baffling them with jargon, you'll have to forgive me always referring to footballers as 'he'. I know that I shouldn't do it, but I feared that if every hypothetical situation became 'and then he/she will take the corner, looking to find the head of the targetman/woman,' it would swiftly become a nightmare.

For the record, I enjoy and respect the women's game and that's the truth, it has nothing to do with the fact that Charlotte, my publisher, is a right-back of fearsome reputation who carves notches on her boots for every ankle she breaks. Not a bit of it. No siree.

I've also tried to make all the real-life examples in this book timeless, so don't worry about the identity of these 1980s and 1990s players too much. Not knowing who Brian Kilcline was is not going to prevent you from enjoying football. *Knowing* who Brian Kilcline was and identifying him as the man who was marking you in your next match ... now that would prevent you enjoying football. And if Sir Alex Ferguson or Arsène Wenger has been sacked in the time it took this book to get from my laptop to your lap, then I humbly apologise. When I wrote this, they looked quite secure.

Anyway, what are you doing still reading this? There's a beautiful game to discover.

Iain Macintosh

Why you should like football

I cannot, even for a moment, comprehend what it must be like to be ignorant of football. To spend Saturdays doing 'stuff', rather than hanging on the vidiprinter's every rattle. To amble past packed out pubs in the summer, wondering what on earth everybody is shouting about. To get to April and think about anything other than the relegation dogfight or the race for a European place.

What do you say to strangers when you meet them? What do you discuss? With football, you have something in common with almost everyone you meet. Prospective parents-in-law, bosses, clients, pretty girls, fit men; in the right hands, a love of football can be a passport to acceptance. There are no awkward silences with football in your life and there is not a bad party in the world that can't be saved by an impromptu council of war in the kitchen to discuss England's perpetual left-flank deficiencies.

Football is a universal language, one so powerful that sometimes it even surpasses the reach of actual languages. I once survived an hour-long taxi ride in Madrid by playing name-tennis with the non-English speaking driver. 'Beckham?'

I said. 'Si, bueno!' Excellent, fifteen-love. 'McManaman?' I ventured. 'Si, mucho bueno!' Thirty-love. 'Thomas Gravesen?' The car stopped abruptly. Tumbleweed bounced slowly across the road. Match forfeited and an important lesson learned.

It is physically impossible to ever run out of things to say about football. There has never yet been a conversation about it that has ended with the words 'Well, I think that just about covers it, what shall we talk about now?' No matter who you support, or what game you've just watched, there's always more to discuss, always players to compare, managers to criticise and clubs to deride.

It's an ever-changing, perpetually evolving soap opera with more twists and turns than anything that the scriptwriters of *EastEnders* and *Coronation Street* could come up with, even on one of their good days when they've got fresh coffee and doughnuts and one of them has been on holiday and had loads of really good ideas on the beach. Only football could create a character as terrifying as Roy Keane, or as loveable as Jimmy Bullard. Only football could make you care about what happens to them, even after they finish their playing careers.

Football should be predictable but, as my bookmaker will tell you from his villa in Tuscany, it never, ever is. Who on earth would have thought that a distinctly average Liverpool side, 0-3 down at half-time in the European Cup Final, could come back and beat a stellar AC Milan outfit on penalties? Who could have foreseen Cameroon overturning the World Champions Argentina, Diego Maradona and all? It's eleven against eleven and, even with 89 of the 90 minutes gone, with one team clearly in control of the game, you never know what will happen. It only takes a moment to score a goal.

Football will bring you incomparable highs and gut-wrenching lows. It will force you to align your consciousness with a motley collection of young men that you'll probably never even meet, sharing their hopes and dreams as the years roll on. Under the flag of your team, you'll be adopted by a new family, drawn from all sections of society, from all over the world. With football, you're never alone and there's never nothing on the television.

The trouble is, as I'm sure you've already found out, it's actually quite difficult to make a late entrance into the fold. Football fans are notoriously sniffy and they don't take kindly to newcomers. Once you've proven yourself worthy, you'll be welcomed with open arms, but how can you prove yourself worthy when no one will explain the simple things that everyone else seems to take for granted? When you keep hearing the phrases 'dropping deep' and 'pushing up', but you're not entirely sure what they mean? When that bloody offside trap continues to confuse you?

There is a certain snobbery in football that prevents people from asking the simple questions for fear of ridicule. This book will save you the trouble. Within these pages you'll find out all you need to know to walk into that pub with confidence, to go to a game and proudly shout abuse at the referee, just like everybody else. All of the basics are here, but without the cold technical language that only makes it more confusing. It's a simple game, and this book is intended to keep it that way.

You'll probably already have heard of Bobby Moore and George Best or Brian Clough and Bill Shankly, but now you'll know what it was they did that was so special that, even before you found football, you knew their names. Most importantly of all, you'll know in your heart which team you should be supporting and why just choosing the most successful team at the time is a no-no.

I don't want to over-egg the pudding or anything, but seriously ... this book is your ticket to a better life.

The history of football

Although it took a combination of Gazza's tears, Nick Hornby, Sky Sports and Baddiel & Skinner to bring football kicking and screaming into the mass market, the game itself has been in existence for much, much, longer than that. Since the dawn of time, mankind has harboured a primal urge to kick stuff, preferably while drinking. Football was its inevitable evolutionary companion.

The first records of a football-like game come from an old Chinese military manual thought to date back to the third century BC. Tsu Chu, a catchy little name that roughly translates to 'kickball', was a ludicrously difficult game that, nevertheless, was extremely popular in the Tsin and Han dynasties. The object of the game was to kick a ball stuffed with fur or feathers into a net approximately 10 or 16in in diameter. The only catch was that the net was suspended on 30ft tall bamboo canes. Apparently, this game was often played as part of the emperor's birthday celebrations, so the next time you think you're stressed, imagine trying to impress a quick-tempered despot by punting a football through a basketball hoop hanging off the top of your house. You wouldn't want to get that wrong too many times.

Over in Japan, somewhere between 300AD and 600AD, they played Kemari, a simple but addictive game played with a ball made from deerskin and sawdust. The object here was for a small team of players, eight or fewer, to keep the ball airborne for as long as they could, essentially like a group version of keepy-ups. You can still see this game being played today by eager-to-impress young men on Spanish beaches, usually within the eyeline of a group of sunbathing girls. Kemari remained popular in Japan for well over a thousand years and pops up regularly in poems and folklore. One legend tells of an emperor who led his team to a mind-boggling 1,000 keepy-ups before retiring the ball and promoting it to a high-ranking position within his court. That's the equivalent of Queen Elizabeth II insisting that her tennis racket is appointed Foreign Secretary.

These, however, are all mere variants of the game we know and love today. For the first example of a competitive team game with a clear objective, we must look to 9th century England, where the first reference of a group of boys 'playing ball' is made. Though this is the first recorded mention of the game, it is highly unlikely to be the first time it was actually played. The most appealing explanation for English football's origin is the theory that the game was played hundreds of years prior to that.

Apparently it was victorious Anglo-Saxon warriors who started it all by enjoying what can only have been a short-lived and particularly messy kickabout with the severed head of a Danish prince. There are other more boring theories about football's origins lying in primitive village festivals with the ball representing the sun and the players attempting to gain supremacy over it to ensure a good harvest, but they're no fun so we'll ignore them entirely.

Medieval football, with actual balls rather than heads, was a violent and chaotic affair. There were no limits on numbers, so the game would be contested by vast mobs across huge swathes of land. Like any game whose only two rules are 'No murder and no manslaughter,' it was low on technical skill and high on blood and gore, a lot like today's Scottish Premier League. If the game was ever played in a town, the players would rip through the streets like a sweaty whirlwind, causing untold damage to property. Unsurprisingly, the authorities began to take rather a dim view of this new pastime.

In 1314, football was officially banned by Edward II, who said he was appalled by the 'great noise in the city caused by hustling over large balls.' Still, at least he invented the double-entendre in the process. He wasn't the only one to despair at the great unwashed and their new hobby. Edward III, Richard II, Henry IV and Henry VIII all tried to put an end to the beautiful game, but the people were not having any of it. Football was fast becoming the national game and the bans were working as effectively as sticking plasters on gunshot wounds.

It wasn't until Oliver Cromwell came to power in 1653 that the sport, such as it was, was really threatened. The old Puritan took such a dim view of anything that might be considered fun that he even banned Christmas, so the chances of him getting involved in a knockabout in the park were always a bit limited. Unfortunately for him, the people latched on to illegal football as a symbol for their rejection of Cromwell's values. In spite of numerous threats to put all participants in the stocks, something which I only wish had been applied to the 2006 England World Cup squad, illegal protest games were organised across the country, especially on Christmas Day, the lack of which was still really bugging them. Cromwell died in 1658 and, entertainingly, his body was dug up by Charles II in 1660 and tried for treason. Unsurprisingly, given that it can't have put up too much of a defence, the corpse was found guilty and beheaded. That'll teach him.

By the 19th century, a number of public schoolmasters were cottoning on to the idea that team games could be used to improve the attitude, work-rate, fitness and character of their students. The anarchic melee of primitive football needed to be codified, but there were two rather major problems. Some people didn't see anything wrong with carrying the ball and others resisted the attempts to remove some of the violence from the game. These people are now called 'rugby fans' and in 1863, when the first official rules of Association Football were drawn up, they stormed out to invent their own game.

The FA Cup was created in 1872 and was won by Wanderers, a team who were originally called Forest FC and were formed in Leytonstone, but 'wandered' over to Battersea a year after formation. In 1888, the first League title was contested and won at a canter by Preston North End who repeated the feat in 1889. The Preston board of directors, by now thinking that this football lark was easy, demanded that a splendid trophy be forged for the winners, instead of the fabric pennants that they had received two years in a row. The Football Association (FA) agreed, but poor old Preston never won the title again.

Football, along with everything else, came to a shuddering halt in 1914 with the outbreak of war, but something extraordinary is said to have happened at Armentières on the first Christmas Day of the conflict. With English and German troops lined up opposite each other in the trenches, the fighting stopped when the Germans began to sing Christmas carols. The English joined in and then one very brave and trusting chap clambered over the top of the fortifications to share his chocolate with the enemy. With bilingual squaddies in short supply, it wasn't long before the international language of football took over. War was suspended and an international match broke out in its place. With crippling inevitability, Germany won the game 3-2, although whether penalties were required goes sadly unrecorded. After a day of humanity, normal hellish service was resumed on Boxing Day when, after a symbolic pistol-shot to open proceedings, both teams reluctantly returned to slaughtering each other.

In 1930, with one war over and another still to come, the first World Cup was held in Uruguay. Unfortunately, the English FA had fallen out with the world governing body FIFA and didn't even enter a team. In fact, it wasn't until after the Second World War that the English rejoined the organisation, making their debut on the world stage in 1950 in Brazil. It was here that the Three Lions served notice of their future ineptitude by contriving to lose to an American team so unfancied that when the 1-0 result was telegrammed to a London newspaper, the sub-editor assumed that it must be a mistake and printed the much more likely scoreline of 1-10.

Much better was to come in 1966 when England hosted the World Cup for the first time and actually won it at Wembley, beating the Germans, or the West Germans as they were then, 4-2. West Ham's Geoff Hurst hit the only hat-trick ever scored in a World Cup Final, West Ham's Martin Peters added another and West Ham's Bobby Moore lifted the trophy. This is why West Ham fans are best avoided, as they tend to go on about it rather a lot.

The 1960s saw the start of a golden age in English football although, interestingly enough, it was led by two Scotsmen.

Manchester United manager Matt Busby was almost killed in the Munich air disaster of 1958 which took the lives of several of his players, but he recovered and rebuilt the club, winning the European Cup ten years later at Wembley. Meanwhile, over in Liverpool, Bill Shankly's team were setting down the foundations for what would be three decades of unparalleled success in domestic and European competition. From 1977, English teams would win that much-coveted European Cup seven years out of the next eight, but then it all came grinding to a halt.

The emergence of widespread football hooliganism threatened to send the game back to the dark ages. Football 'firms' clashed repeatedly up and down the country, battling for dominance and feeding off their own legends. Pitch invasions were such a regular occurrence that special fences had to be put up to pen people in. Stabbings and beatings were rife, as were assaults on police officers and damage to private property. It was even worse when English teams travelled to play in Europe. Historic cities would brace themselves as if the Mongols had been sighted on the borders, and with good reason. It all came to a head at the 1985 European Cup Final in Heysel, Belgium, when 39 Italian fans were killed following clashes with Liverpool supporters. It was the final straw for the authorities and English clubs were banned from European competition for an indefinite period. UEFA eventually allowed them back after five years, with the exception of Liverpool who served a further year for their part in the disaster.

Hooligans were not the only problem. The nation's stadiums were decrepit and utterly unsuitable for the modern game. A fire at Valley Parade in Bradford in 1985 killed 56 people, but worse came four years later at Hillsborough in

Sheffield when 96 Liverpool fans were crushed to death on the Leppings Lane terraces. The fences that had been erected to stop hooligans from invading the pitch killed innocent supporters instead.

In the aftermath of the tragedy, the government appointed Lord Taylor of Gosforth to oversee an inquiry into its causes and to make recommendations on ways of avoiding its recurrence. The Taylor Report of 1990 stipulated that all stadiums in the top two divisions were to be converted into all-seater arenas, cutting out the possibility of overcrowding and making violence in the stands almost impossible. The fences came down, alcohol sales were regulated and football stadiums became altogether nicer places to visit. Attendances, which had been dropping steadily, began to rise again, as women, children and people of all ethnic backgrounds began to tentatively dangle their toes in what had always been a no-go area for them.

In 1992, everything changed. A breakaway group of clubs formed the Premier League in an effort to secure a greater share of television revenues. Sky Sports paid them an enormous sum of money for the screening rights and promptly revolutionised the way that the country watched football by broadcasting it on what felt like a near-constant basis. The extra money led to astronomical rises in players' wages and the arrival of some of the world's biggest stars, who came because they loved England and absolutely not because they wanted to make a quick buck before they retired.

Now the Premier League is arguably the greatest league in world football. The stadiums are magnificent, the quality is exquisite and some of the best players on earth are here out of choice and not just because it's the best way to sort a tricky alimony payment. We've come a long way since Tsu Chu. Imagine all that history, all those teams and all those players all leading up to this one moment in time. The moment when you decided you wanted to take an interest in football. Makes the back of your neck tingle, doesn't it?

Aren't you glad you picked up this book? Of course you are! Come on, let's find out how it all works.

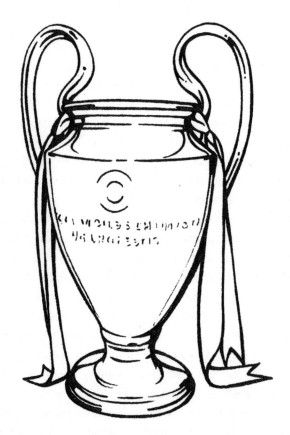

3

The basics

The players

Football is a game contested by two teams of eleven players on a big pitch which, with a bit of luck, is covered in short, green grass and not festooned with dog poo and broken bottles. That just ruins it for everyone. You'll find a goal at both ends of the pitch and, as any fool knows, the object of the game is, quite simply, to get the ball in the goal, while preventing your opponents from putting it in yours.

Unless you're the goalkeeper, who we'll come to later, you can use any part of your body to manoeuvre the ball around except your arms and hands. It's not unusual to see the ball kicked up in the air by one player, met by the head of another and then brought under control with the chest of a third. Goals have been scored with kneecaps, bottoms and even, painfully, with faces. It's only the arms and hands that are a no-no. Diego Maradona once put England out of a World Cup by punching the ball into the net without the referee noticing and he still hasn't been forgiven for it.

Now, there are a few basic terms that we need to get out of the way to prevent you working your way down the page and crying out in ignorant frustration. You might know some of these already, in which case feel free to skim-read, I won't be offended. Kicking the ball to one of your team-mates is known as a 'pass', running with the ball at your feet is 'dribbling', kicking the ball at the goal is generally called a 'shot', any contact between ball and head is a 'header' and attempting to dispossess your opponent by kicking or blocking the ball with your feet is called a 'tackle'. Got that? Of course you have, you look the clever type.

For ease of understanding, I'm going to split the players into three distinct groups: defenders, midfielders and attackers. Most teams play with a formation of one goalkeeper, four defenders, four midfielders and two attackers, but there are no rules governing the quotas. If a manager wants to play with one goalkeeper and ten attackers then he is very welcome, but don't expect him to win too many games. Balance is the key.

Defenders are there to stop the other team from scoring. They tend to remain in their own half of the pitch, guarding their goal. They'll tackle anyone who comes near and head away any balls that are kicked up in the air in their direction. They are usually physically stronger and larger than the majority of the other players, but there are exceptions. Of the four defenders, the ones on either side, towards the edges of the pitch, are known as 'full-backs', either 'left-back' or 'right back' depending on their location, and perform much the same role, but many of them are asked to run forwards and help out the midfielders as well.

Sometimes defenders can disrupt players even if they're nowhere near the ball, by standing very close to their opponent and discouraging his team-mates from passing to him, following him everywhere he goes. No one wants to risk giving the ball to someone with a defender all over him like a rash. This socially acceptable form of stalking is called 'marking' and we'll go into more depth on it later.

Midfielders are generally the most versatile of footballers. They help out the defenders by trying to tackle their opponents in the middle of the pitch, but their main objective is to pass the ball to the attackers. Size isn't too important here, but they do need to be capable of all the basic skills, especially if they are positioned in the centre of the pitch. Some midfielders are ordered to stay out on the flanks. These chaps are called 'wingers' and they tend to be very fast and very good at kicking the ball in the air towards the goal from the edges of the pitch, a special pass known as a 'cross'.

Attackers, or strikers as they are often known, are the stars of the show. Their job is to kick or head the ball into the goal. Defenders will try and tackle them and they'll almost certainly be outnumbered, but if they can just put that ball in the goal, they'll get bought lots of drinks and girls will like them more. You get tall ones who specialise in heading the wingers' crosses in and little quick ones who specialise in making defenders look silly by running past them with the ball. As it is goals that win games, attackers are valued more than other players and, if you ever see a list of the supposed best footballers in the world, the vast majority will be attackers.

Goalkeepers are a completely different animal altogether. They even wear a different coloured kit to distinguish themselves. They can use their hands, but only in the penalty area which, for those who don't know, is that big white box around the goal, also known enigmatically as 'the box' or descriptively as 'the 18-yard box'. If an attacker shoots at goal and they catch it or deflect it away, it's called a 'save'. Being able to jump in the air and pluck the ball out of the sky means that any passes that are kicked up in the air are at risk of being snaffled away, so midfielders have to be careful. Goalkeepers are almost always tall with hands the size of dinner plates and the reactions of a particularly tense cat in Battersea Dogs Home.

Every team has a selection of spare players that they can bring on as replacements during the course of the game. These poor lost souls are called substitutes, or 'subs' for short. Their fate is to sit on the sidelines, upon the fabled 'bench' that you'll hear mentioned so often, and wait to be allowed to play. Three factors could lead to their involvement. There could be an injury so serious that it necessitates a replacement, there could be an individual performance so abject that the manager is forced to haul the miscreant off the pitch and give someone else a go, or it could be a tactical decision. If a team is losing the game, the manager may decide to do something drastic like taking off a defender to replace him with another attacker.

Injuries aside, changes tend not to happen until the game is in its later stages. This is why footballers are so unhappy to be 'left on the bench'. It means that they probably won't get to play and, even if they do, it won't be for very long.

The pitch and passages of play

All football matches begin with a kick-off, which takes place in that circle in the centre of the pitch, conveniently known as the 'centre circle'. A coin is tossed by the referee before the game and the two team captains call to see who will open proceedings. The team designated to start must wait for the referee to blow his whistle before kicking the ball forwards and beginning the game. None of their opponents can enter the centre circle until the ball is touched by two players, which is why you always see footballers lined up on the edge of it, ready to pounce.

The vast majority of kick-offs result in a period of passes, tackles, headers and occasionally even a shot before someone inevitably kicks or heads the ball beyond those touchlines that border the pitch on both sides and at either end. If the ball runs off the pitch at the sides, the game is stopped and restarted with a 'throw-in'. One player, always from the team who didn't send the ball will step forwards, grab the ball in both hands and hurl it over his head, back into play, whereupon the game will start again.

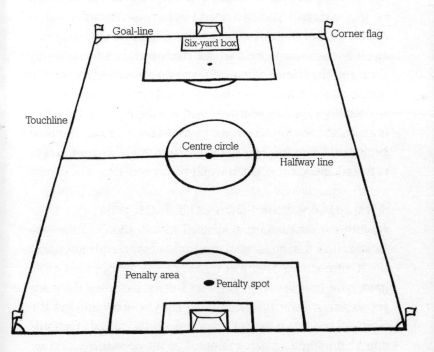

Fig. 1 The areas of a football pitch

Throw-ins are usually straightforward affairs barely worthy of a mention, but there are some teams well-equipped enough to use them to their advantage. A quick throw-in can catch a distracted team off guard and lead to a shooting opportunity, while a long one can cause absolute chaos. Any team with tall attackers will always try to get the ball high into the penalty area at every opportunity, because their strikers will be able to jump above the defenders and head the ball at goal. If your team is blessed with a man who can chuck a football like a cannon fires a circus midget, and a couple of chaps who can reach the top shelves in the supermarket without going on tiptoes, then throw-ins are going to come in rather handy.

Throw-ins can also be a good escape route for an attacking move that has run out of momentum. Imagine that you're a quick winger, running down the pitch with the ball. As you approach the corner of the penalty area, you spot a defender running towards you. You want to pass the ball to a team-mate, but all the other defenders are marking them, so it's probably not a good idea. You're struggling for breath and you can hear another defender running up behind you. Now, you don't want to be tackled by either of them and you can't see anyone to pass to, so you cleverly tap the ball forwards at the incoming defender and watch it bounce off his shins and out over the touchline. Congratulations, you've just 'bought a throw-in'. Time to find that bloke who can sling it into the penalty area.

Of course, you can't just throw it in willy-nilly. The taker must have both feet on the ground, must be facing the pitch and must throw the ball with both hands from behind, straight over his own head. Failure to do it properly results in a 'foul-throw', the throw-in being awarded to the opposition, and an invitation to widespread contempt for the foul-thrower.

Now, imagine that you were not anywhere near crafty enough to 'buy a throw-in' and that you carried on running, zipping past that defender and going straight over the far touchline, the one that runs along the line of the goal. If you, or a member of your team, ever put the ball past that line then the game stops and the ball is given to the goalkeeper for a 'goal-kick'. The goalkeeper will put the ball down on either corner of that very small box inside the penalty area, known as 'the six-yard box', and then he'll run up and kick it back into play. The ball must leave the penalty area before any of his team-mates can touch it, so the goalkeeper needs to make sure he gets a bit of distance on it at the very least.

A long goal-kick can also be a useful weapon, but only if it's accurate. There's no point in getting the ball back only to blast it all the way down the pitch to the other goalkeeper. A well-aimed kick, perhaps to one of your tall attackers, can be just the thing to start another attacking move. It doesn't have to be a long kick though. Many teams prefer to ensure that they'll keep possession of the ball by just passing it to the nearest team-mate. After all, their opponents can't score if they haven't got the ball, can they?

Now, let's go back to you running down that wing. If, instead of buying a throw-in or running off the pitch like Forrest Gump, you had tried to kick it towards the penalty area, hit that defender in the leg and seen the ball run over the touchline behind the goal, you'd have won your team a 'corner'. Corners are part of the 'set-piece' family, moments in the game that start at the blow of a whistle rather than developing from open play and, as a result, can be carefully planned.

Corners are awarded whenever the ball crosses the far touchline immediately after making contact with one of your opponents and they're very important. You, or one of your team-mates, will put the ball down in the tiny circle in front of the corner flag and kick it into the penalty area. None of the opposition can come within ten yards of the corner-taker before he touches the ball, so there's enough time to take a breath and think carefully about the best place to deliver it.

Most teams will have specific plans for attacking and defending corners, usually involving those tall players again. The attacking team might move two tall players to either post, but they will usually be followed by two members of the defending team, designated to mark them at these moments. There is usually a delay before the corner is taken when you'll have the chance to watch up to twenty-two men scattering backwards, forwards and side-to-side in what looks like the most messily choreographed ballet in history. Don't worry; this is entirely normal. Some players will even be told to run in a direction where they're never going to get the ball, purely to confuse the defenders. A well-taken corner can be placed on the head of a tall attacker for him to head into the goal. A poor one can go straight to a defender or even, in the most risible of cases, straight off the pitch. Like everything in football, practice makes perfect.

Football matches last for 90 minutes, split into two halves and broken up by a 15-minute interval known as 'half-time'. The referee may decide to play longer if he feels that the game has been delayed by injuries or time-wasting. Just before both half-time and full-time you'll see one of the referee's assistants holding up a board with a number on it. This is the minimum amount of time that should be added on, known as 'injury time'.

At half-time, the players will scurry off down the tunnel towards their dressing rooms for a cup of tea or an isotonic drink and the congratulations or fury of their manager. When they return, the two teams will swap ends and play in the other direction. This is to make sure that any adverse conditions, such as bright sunshine in the eyes or strong winds, are experienced by both teams.

Fouls and free-kicks

Despite the best efforts of those 19th century football rule-makers, the dark arts of kicking, tripping, pushing and hitting did not leave the game with the fathers of rugby. 'Fouling' is as much a part of football now as it was in the early days of the sport. Sometimes the fouls are accidental, but often the only way to stop that attacker is to kick his feet out from under him and send him tumbling to the ground. It's just good sense.

The standard punishment for a foul is a free-kick to the opposition. The only exception is if the offence occurs in the penalty area, in which case it's a penalty kick, but more on that later. There are dozens of ways to foul your opponent, so let's have a look at them.

Tripping an opponent is obviously out, as is kicking them up in the air like a pile of leaves, but if the defender can make contact with the ball before the man, referees tend to be a bit more lenient. This doesn't mean that the defender can slide into the ball and then cripple the attacker by following through, it just means that the officials need to see that the intention was to tackle and not to maim. Often you'll see footballers jumping up after executing a heavy tackle and desperately pointing at the ball's sudden change of direction. This would indicate that their tackle was fair.

Direct free-kicks	Indirect free-kicks	Goalkeepers only
• Kicking an opponent	• Obstructing an opponent by standing in front of him and being awkward	• Having the ball in his hands for more than six seconds before releasing it
• Tripping an opponent	• Playing in a dangerous manner, perhaps by kicking your legs high in the air	• Touching the ball with his hands again after releasing it. You can't pick the ball up for a bit, put it down, wait for an attacker to come near you, and snatch it back off the floor
• Jumping or charging at an opponent		
• Punching, slapping or whacking an opponent on the head	• Preventing the goalkeeper from releasing the ball from his hands	
• Pushing an opponent	• Unsporting behaviour (e.g. shouting "leave it," which can confuse players)	• Picking up or palming away a back pass
• Tackling the opponent before making contact with the ball	• Clambering all over an opponent's back in an effort to gain a height advantage for a header etc.	• Picking up or palming away a throw-in
• Holding an opponent		
• Deliberately handling the ball	• Deceit (e.g. diving)	
• Spitting at an opponent	• To restart the game after a caution for dissent/ a sending-off for foul language/an offside decision etc.	

Free-kicks are either direct, which means you can have a shot at goal, or indirect, which means you have to pass it to someone before you can open fire. The easiest way to remember the difference is that (D)irect free-kicks are given for (D)eeds and (I)ndirect free-kicks are given for (I)nfractions. Kick a man in the ankles, that's a deed. Obstruct a man, that's an infraction. Elbow your marker in the nose, that's a deed. Stand in front of the goalkeeper while he's trying to throw the ball out, that's an infraction. Opposite is a list to help.

It's worth taking a moment to clarify the handball rule, which is a constant source of confusion for fans. Handball itself is not actually an offence, 'deliberate handball' is the crime. If a ball is kicked hard at a player's hand, it's not necessarily a foul. There has to be an intention to control or block the ball for the free-kick or penalty to be awarded. The player has to make an effort to get his grubby mitts out of the way, but if the pace of the ball makes that impossible, it is colloquially known as 'ball-to-hand' and the game continues.

Most free-kicks are like most throw-ins: entirely uneventful ways of restarting the game. However, if a free-kick is given near the edge of the penalty area, it becomes something different entirely. A direct free-kick within, say, 25 or 35 yards of the goal is a shooting opportunity, one so dangerous that the defending side will build a human 'wall' in an effort to stop the ball. They can only stand as near as 10 yards to the taker, but they'll link arms, grit their teeth and hold steady as the free-kick is blasted towards them. Well, some will. Some footballers will take the understandable precaution of clasping their hands over their more vulnerable places, while some big Jessies will even turn around to make sure they don't get hit in the face.

Over the years a number of players, among them Matthew Le Tissier, David Beckham and Cristiano Ronaldo, have made names for themselves by being free-kick specialists. For them, a wall means nothing. If a ball is kicked in the right way it can be curled around the defenders, or even up over their heads and back down into the goal. But direct free-kicks can be as doltish as they can be deadly. For every curled ripsnorter of a shot that whistles over the wall and into the top corner, another ten will be driven into the midriff of a defender, or powered high into the stands behind the goal.

If an offence takes place in the penalty area, a 'penalty' is awarded and this is where the fun begins. Penalties, or 'spot kicks' as they can be known, are moments of great drama when an attacking player is given a free, unopposed shot at goal from the spot in the centre of the penalty area. Everyone else has to clear out and leave the attacker and the goalkeeper to their duel. The referee will blow the whistle and the attacker will have one shot to score. He can't dribble it, there is little advantage in passing it and all the pressure is on him to beat the keeper. If the ball hits the post or the goalkeeper, anyone can run in and smash home the rebound, but until the ball is kicked, no one else is allowed in the penalty area.

Sometimes footballers will celebrate the award of a penalty almost as if it's a goal because it is so likely to actually result in one. This almost literal definition of hubris is considered poor form by more mature observers, but it can be very amusing if the eventual spot kick is missed.

Goalkeepers love penalties because it's the one occasion in the game when they can't be held accountable. Theoretically, it is so simple for a footballer to score a goal from a spot kick that they are never blamed if the ball goes past them. If they move in the right direction and save the ball, they're the hero. If not, it's hardly their fault, is it?

This is precisely why penalties are so interesting. You get to watch a highly paid professional attempt to undertake an ordinary task under extraordinary pressure. That goal can look terribly small sometimes...

Goals

Everything in football is geared towards one objective: scoring goals. I've spoken to goalscorers from the lower leagues, the foreign leagues and the Premier League and they've all told me the same thing. I've even spoken to Pelé himself and he's confirmed it. There is nothing quite like scoring a goal. Watching the ball flash away from your outstretched boot, hearing the ripple of the net before the roar of the crowd, losing all sensation in your legs as your team-mates bundle you to the ground and scream in your ears. It's what the game is all about.

A goal is awarded if the entire ball crosses the line that runs from one goalpost to another. Note the use of the word 'entire'. Just having the ball touch the line, or even leaning almost over it isn't good enough. The whole of the ball must enter the goal. England took a decisive lead in the 1966 World Cup Final with a ferocious shot that ... well, don't tell anyone I said this, but it probably didn't cross the line. We owe the proudest moment in our sporting history to a generous Azerbaijani linesman. I've always liked Azerbaijan. Incidentally, this chap is often referred to as 'The Russian Linesman', a misnomer since the end of the Cold War and those shifting national borders. Feel free to correct people with a tut and a sad shake of the head.

The wonderful thing about goals is that they count the same no matter how they are scored. You can dribble the ball past every member of the opposition team, flick it up in the air and overhead kick it into the top corner of the net from 30 yards out, but it will mean as much as a deflected long shot that smacks you in the face and dribbles over the line. It is for this reason that football is so compelling because it means that talent and technique can never completely dominate. In the 1980s, a number of teams prospered by putting lots of very big, very quick attackers on the pitch and kicking the ball high into the air all the time, preventing the prettier, shorter teams from being able to settle into their routine of short, crisp passes. This 'route one' football wasn't very popular because it made such awful viewing, but it won a lot of games.

Far better though are the goals that are so emphatic that they have you leaping out of your seat in surprise. Any shot struck from outside the penalty area is always nice, but anything that hits the back of the net while still rising and accelerating deserves special mention. There's always a place in my heart for a diving header and overhead kicks are a rare gem. Then there are the solo efforts where one player tears down the pitch on his own and you're waiting for him to pass it or lose it, but he keeps the ball and gleefully slams it home without any help from anyone. The team movements where the ball is pinged about the pitch 20 or 30 times before being dispatched with aplomb, the stunning shots from narrow angles, the delicate lobs and chips. You'll never get bored of goals.

One type of goal that is never included in this pantheon of greatness is the 'own-goal'. There is little in football as humiliating as scoring in the wrong net, though clemency can occasionally be granted depending on the circumstances. It's hard to blame a defender who valiantly sprints back towards his own goal and slides in to block a shot, but inadvertently knocks it over the line instead. Less sympathy is granted to the blundering numbnuts who power headers past their own goalkeepers or who chip passes into their own net. However, like the 30-yard exocet and the 2-yard header, it all counts for the same in the end. Many a game has been won and lost on one poor sod's individual moment of lunacy.

Sometimes a goal can be disallowed. This is a uniquely disappointing moment, usually met with howls and jeers from the supporters of the wronged team and a volley of abuse towards the officials from the players. Goals can be disallowed for a number of reasons, most commonly for 'offside', but you're not ready for that little headache just yet. Others have perished for fouls in the build-up, perhaps a push on a defender from an attacker stretching for a header, or even for a tug on the shirt of a marker to prevent him from jumping at a team-mate. The officials are always on the lookout for indiscretions so be careful when you celebrate. I once leapt up in a pub and screamed something very rude about Portugal and the legitimacy of their footballers' birth certificates before someone pointed out that the goal had been disallowed for a push. I beg you not to share my shame.

However, if you see the ball in the back of the net and you don't see the referee fending off a phalanx of furious footballers, then you can assume that everything is a-ok. You'll know that everything is alright when you see the referee blowing his whistle and pointing at the centre circle. When the goalscorer has finally finished dancing with the corner flag, the game is restarted with a kick-off, which is precisely where we started this exhaustive run through of the basics of football and, indeed, it is where we shall end it.

Congratulations, you now know everything you need to know to enjoy a game of football on a basic level. No longer will you be troubled by 'walls', 'marking' and 'own-goals'. No more will you ponder the difference between an indirect and a direct free kick. You're well on your way, but there is still far to travel. Get yourself a cup of tea and meet me at the next chapter, the tricky bits. It's time for the next stage of your training.

4
The tricky bits

Back passes

Back in the 1980s, Liverpool were arguably the best football team in Europe and it wasn't because they had more money than anyone else, or anything silly like that. Strong foundations had been set down by Bill Shankly, built upon by Bob Paisley and continued by Joe Fagan and Kenny Dalglish. Liverpool did all the simple things well. They passed the ball accurately, defended well and made sure that they took their chances. They believed in themselves, fought for each other and set high standards that, by and large, they usually met. But they were crafty buggers as well.

Liverpool believed fervently in the maxim that the other team cannot score if they haven't got the ball and as a result they were very careful with their passes. They also knew, as you do now, that their goalkeeper could pick up the ball. With that in mind it was quite common to see them take the lead and then slowly pass the ball around the pitch, making their opponents chase round in circles like piggies in the middle. If the situation got too risky, the ball would be passed back to their goalkeeper who would pick it up and then dawdle around the penalty area for a while. He would then roll the ball back out to his defenders who might pass the ball up and down the edge of the penalty area for 30 seconds before knocking it back to the goalkeeper again to restart the whole, brain-meltingly dull process. Liverpool won an awful lot of games because their opponents got bored and went home. Metaphorically, at least.

They weren't the only ones. Arsenal, under the dour George Graham, were exactly the same, as were many others. If in doubt, cautious managers instructed their players to 'just knock the ball back to your goalkeeper so that he can pick it up'. It was safe, it was secure, it was reeeeally boring.

The final straw came after the 1990 World Cup was marred by repeated back passes and time-wasting. FIFA, who you will recall are football's world governing body, were appalled. They were desperately trying to market the beautiful game and it was being made to look distinctly ugly by the so-called best footballers in the world. In 1992, they cracked and outlawed the back pass to the goalkeeper. It remains the single most successful and popular piece of FIFA legislation in living memory.

Goalkeepers could still pick up the ball if it was headed back, or chested back, but if it was deliberately passed back by the feet of a team-mate, then he was in a bit of a situation. You see, goalkeepers, in all but the rarest of cases, are dreadful footballers. They choose to play in goal as children because they're simply not good enough in any other position and it's the only way they'll get to be involved in a football match. For them, the sight of a swiftly moving football being passed back towards them is like seeing a big, grey fin in the water.

The first few years after the rule was introduced were

a golden period for slapstick comedy. Goalkeepers across the world were forced to control footballs with their feet and the learning curve was steep and unforgiving. Back passes were scuffed into the stands, driven into the ground and inadvertently given to opposing attackers. Crowds roared with laughter as highly paid professional athletes went into a very public panic, melting at the sight of the key tool of their trade. Air-kicks, once the sole province of wobbling toddlers and habitual drunks, were commonplace. It was a wonderful time to be alive.

Sadly, the goalkeepers eventually evolved and the mistakes were slowly reduced, if not completely eradicated. These days, coaches get hold of them at a very young age and teach them what their predecessors missed out on: how to kick a moving ball.

If the referee judges that a goalkeeper has picked up a deliberate back pass from a member of his own team, he awards an indirect free-kick (it's an infraction rather than a deed) on the spot where he touched the ball with his hands. In most cases, this is inside the penalty area, which has led to some very strange free-kicks. Remember that an indirect free-kick cannot just be blasted towards the goal. It has to be touched by someone else first. There is also that wall to contend with. As most offences occur within 10 yards of the goal, the defenders are forced to huddle on the goal-line itself. What you get, in these very rare occurrences, is a kind of human shooting gallery. The free-kick taker will tap the ball to his team-mate, usually the one with the hardest shot, the defenders will charge off the line towards him and shortly afterwards you'll hear the sickening thud of leather on flesh, followed by a pitiful whimpering sound.

There are occasions where the goalkeeper can pick the ball up and not be penalised. These include deflections and wild clearances that veer off in the wrong direction. The referee is under instruction to only penalise a deliberate back pass. If the defender was trying to kick the ball somewhere else and it ended up going backwards to the goalkeeper then no offence has been committed. It might be worth finding a new defender though.

Since the back pass was abolished, football has become faster and more exciting. Goalkeepers have had to improve their distribution of the ball and there is no longer a hiding place for defenders. Interestingly, Liverpool have yet to win a league title with the new rules in place. I'm sure it can't be just because of that though ... can it?

Offside

For any newcomer to football, understanding the offside rule isn't simply a litmus test of your progress. It's the marble gateway silently guarding the kingdom of the beautiful game. Actually, scratch that, it's the gargoyle on top of the marble gateway. You know, the one that threatens to vaporise those who are not pure of heart. It is a sobering fact that generations of young football fans have been lost to the game, destroyed by the probing cruelty of their first inquisition.

'Come on then,' someone will eventually sneer at you. 'Explain the offside rule.'

Now, before 2005 this was actually a lot easier than you might think, but we'll come to that in due course. Let's start at the beginning. The rule was originally introduced in an effort to combat something which, in my schoolyard, was known as 'goal-hanging'. Think of how simple football would be if you could go wherever you wanted. Devotees of 'route one' football would simply deploy four or five very big men and stand them in a circle around the opposing goalkeeper, waiting for an artillery bombardment of long balls that they could then nod home. It would be rubbish.

Imagine that you're an attacker. The offside rule essentially means that, as that attacker, you cannot stand nearer to the goalkeeper than the most defensive defender when the ball is played. If you imagine the defenders to be arranged in a straight line of four across the edge of the penalty area, facing down the pitch towards the opposition's penalty area, then you should be able to visualise two distinct areas on the pitch. The zone in front of those defenders, or in line with them, is where you would be allowed to stand (onside), and the region behind them is where you could not (offside).

I should point out that, technically, the rule states that you are offside if you are nearer to the goal than the *second last opponent*, but as this usually includes the goalkeeper, it is almost always that most defensive defender.

Pre-2005, you weren't offside until the moment that someone kicked the ball towards you. It was at the moment of delivery, the second that the ball was released, that the judgement was made. If, at that point, you were on the wrong side, nearer to the goal than the most defensive defender, or as they're generally known, 'the last man', then you would have been caught offside and a free-kick awarded against you. The only way of escaping punishment was if you were deemed to be 'not interfering with play'.

Now, as Bill Nicholson, who managed Tottenham to a league and cup double in 1961, once asked, 'If he's not interfering with play, what's he doing on the pitch?' All very amusing and quotable, but it didn't really help. After all, if you're offside on the left flank of the pitch, but the ball is kicked towards your onside strike partner on the right, is it really worth stopping the game? Are you gaining an unfair advantage? Of course not, you haven't even got the ball. You're nowhere near it.

Thus, referees had the power of discretion to decide who was interfering and who wasn't. They still made mistakes, some of them very silly, but by and large everyone knew what the offside rule was essentially all about. *You can't stand nearer to the goal than the last defender and goalkeeper.*

Then in 2005, FIFA started messing around with it. First, they decided that linesman had to wait for an attacking player to touch the ball before flagging, a move that saw officials up and down the country screamed at by furious fans who thought they'd gone to sleep. Then they decided on a new definition of 'phases of play' to 'aid' officials with their decision making.

Here's an extract from a match report in the 2007/8 season when Everton had a goal disallowed under the new offside rule. Don't worry, even I don't fully understand what it says and I actually wrote it.

'It was happening again at the weekend when they (Everton) were denied a perfectly good goal by the Offside Clarification of 2005. Andy Johnson, who scored when he was onside by a comfortable margin, saw his goal ruled out because he was offside in 'the second phase'. The problem, you see, was that Johnson was offside when the move started, but was deemed to be onside because he wasn't interfering with play. Then, when he was onside, he was deemed to be offside, because it was the second phase and despite being offside, but onside, for the first phase, he was onside, but actually offside for the second. Thanks for clarifying that, FIFA. Keep up the good work.'

Are you ok? You might need a sit down after that. The annoying thing is that the new rule actually makes perfect sense, although you will have to trust me on that, but it just doesn't take into account the fact that the poor sods with the flags have to be able to see in three directions at once and memorise the positions of 22 players in a split second. It's asking rather a lot of them and you get the feeling that the rule was 'clarified' by someone who had never actually held a flag in his life.

Anyway, the point is that the offside rule is a very simple one; it's just been twisted beyond recognition in certain areas by the game's lawmakers. If you can learn the basic principle that, *as an attacker, you can't stand closer to the goal than the last defender and goalkeeper when the ball is played*, then that will do for now. Believe it or not, most TV pundits still struggle with

Offside rule

You can't be offside:

- From a throw-in, goal-kick or corner kick
- Inside your own half of the pitch
- When level with the second from last man (including the goalkeeper)
- When level with the last two men
- If the ball is played backwards to you
- If the ball's final touch is from an opponent
- If you're not interfering with play, but let's not go down that road again, eh?

the 'clarification', so you'll just have to join the rest of us, shaking our heads in dismay and wishing for simpler times.

Referees and cards

I've mentioned them a lot already, but it's about time we had a closer look at the match officials. The referee is in charge of the game from some time before the start until just after the finish. He will arrive at the stadium hours before kick-off to make sure everything is ready, occasionally he'll speak to the players and managers beforehand and then he'll run the game and submit a report to the FA at the end before packing up his bag and going home.

Before 2002, all referees were amateurs, paid only expenses and a modest match fee, but the huge influx of money in the game made this quaint state of affairs unsustainable. Referees have so much influence on the game of football that their decisions can mean the success or failure of the clubs that are, essentially, multi-million pound businesses. Also, it was beginning to look a bit silly having schoolteachers and bank managers on £50 a day running around after men who earned that much in five minutes.

Nowadays, most referees are full-time professionals, paid a whopping great retainer ever year with large match fees on top. They deserve it too. Referees lead a thankless existence, always blamed and never congratulated. While we sit at home watching super slow motion replays from 18 different camera angles, they have to make huge decisions in real time, usually while being shouted at by the players and while having very rude songs sung about them by tens of thousands of supporters. The only time they get a laugh is when the ball hits them in the face or if they fall over.

Fortunately, they are given a little bit of help by their two assistants on either touchline. For over a hundred years these chaps were called linesmen because they ran up and down the line waving their flags for offsides. Now, in a stunningly pointless bit of rebranding, they are known as 'assistant referees'. No one knows why. If you want to gain a bit of credibility while watching football, refer to them as linesmen or 'linoes' anyway. People will think you've been watching the game for years.

The linesmen, sorry, assistant referees, are not just limited to offside adjudications. They can also wave their flag to draw the referee's attention to other incidents like fouls, fights or even if objects are being thrown on to the pitch, a depressingly common occurrence. Interestingly, they actually have no real influence on the game. The referee can ignore their signals if he chooses. It's not unknown for a flag to go up for offside and for a referee to signal for the game to continue because he disagrees with his colleague.

Referees don't even have to award the fouls that they do see, if they believe that it will end up punishing the wronged team even further. If you're running past the halfway line and you're fouled by the opposition midfielder, but the ball rolls on to your team-mate who has a chance to score, the referee might decide to 'play the advantage' and allow the game to carry on. Blowing his whistle and awarding the foul would just prevent your team-mate from scoring, so why bother? This doesn't mean that the nefarious midfielder gets away with it though. When the move comes to an end, the referee can call him back and book him for the foul, even if he didn't award the free-kick.

Referees have the ability to dismiss players from the game if they see any serious misbehaviour. Along with his trusty whistle, he will carry a notebook and two coloured cards, one yellow and one red. The yellow card is to signal an official

Yellow card

Players can be cautioned for any of the offences listed below:

- **Unsporting behaviour** This could be anything from taking your shirt off to celebrate a goal, to diving in an attempt to convince the referee that you were fouled. This used to be known as 'ungentlemanly conduct' and still covers some wonderful things like unnecessary shouting.

- **Dissent** This can include backchat, minor swearing, rude names or even sarcasm. Wayne Rooney was once shown a second yellow card for sarcastically applauding the referee's decision to show him a first one.

- **A nasty foul** Technically, this is part of unsporting behaviour, but it's included here just to emphasise that it can only take one foul for a referee to say, "Alright sonny, another one of those and you're off."

- **Persistent fouling** Anyone racking up a series of little, niggly trips can be in the book if the referee catches on quick enough.

- **Time-wasting** "And pick the ball up. And put it down again. And rearrange myself. And fiddle with my hair. And go to kick it. And stop..." And you're booked! No one likes a time-waster.

- **Failure to retreat** All players have to move 10 yards away from a free-kick. Failure to do so after a warning from the referee will result in a sudden flash of yellow cardboard.

- **Entering or re-entering the pitch without permission** You can't just sneak on a substitute while no one is looking. The referee has to be notified of every change.

caution to a player. The red card is to dismiss him from the game entirely. If a player is cautioned and then perpetrates a foul that is worthy of another caution, he is shown a second yellow card and then a red, the concept being that two yellow

Red card

The red card is handed out for the more severe offences, such as:

- **Serious foul play** You don't need to lift both feet off the ground and home in on your opponent's ankles like a heat-seeking missile, you really don't. And it will get you sent off.

- **Violent conduct** Hitting people is definitely out, even if they're on the same team as you. Newcastle United's Lee Bowyer and Kieron Dyer were both sent off in 2005 for scrapping with each other, reducing their team to nine men.

- **Spitting** A disgusting thing to do, but you'd be surprised how often it happens.

- **Denying a goalscoring opportunity with a handball** If your goalkeeper saved the first shot and is lying on the ground, it doesn't mean that you can take over and punch away the second. Some dastardly players used to deliberately save the ball, knowing that they would only see yellow. Not anymore.

- **Denying a goalscoring opportunity with a foul** This is known as a 'professional foul', a last-ditch attempt to stop the striker from scoring, usually executed by a ponderous defender upset at being outpaced by an attacker.

- **Using offensive language or gestures** The referee might be one, but you can't call him one, whatever decisions he gives against you.

cards are worth a single red one. The notebook is for the referee to write down the name and number of the players he cautions, so that he remembers for later. This is why picking up a caution/yellow card is also known as being 'booked'.

When a player is given a red card he must leave the field of play immediately. He is not even allowed to sit on the bench with the substitutes, which is why you will see dismissed footballers storming down the tunnel to the dressing rooms. This is also the reason for the saying 'He's off for an early bath.'

The referee can even send managers, coaches and unused substitutes off, if he decides that they are causing trouble. Managers who lose their tempers and start swearing at the officials are sent directly to the stands, which is always amusing if the game is being held in someone else's stadium. David Moyes, the Everton manager, found this out at the Britannia Stadium in 2008 when the referee told him to go and sit with the Stoke fans. He was not amused.

A football match must be abandoned if a team can no longer field seven players, so too many red cards can end a game. It happened in 2002 when Sheffield United had three men sent off and then lost a further two to injury. With them having just six men on the pitch, the referee was forced to abandon the game.

The final responsibility for a referee is to keep an eye on the conditions. He decides if the pitch is fit to play on before the game and he can abandon it at any point if he feels that it is no longer safe. A sudden outbreak of snow or the steady influx of fog can make a game unplayable in a matter of moments, so he has to be on his guard for every eventuality.

All in all, you can see why they decided to pay them a decent wage, can't you?

The tactics
Formations

It's no good just having talented players, they still need to be deployed correctly across the pitch and tactics are every bit as important to the game of football as technique. The most obvious indicator of a team's tactical set-up is their 'formation'. This will always be a series of numbers that add up to ten, indicating how many defenders, midfielders and attackers are in the team. The goalkeeper isn't included, as we know where he plays. Now, as we've already found, four defenders, four midfielders and two attackers is the usual line-up and would be classed as a 4-4-2. Three defenders, five midfielders and two attackers would therefore be a 3-5-2. Simple, isn't it?

A tactically minded football manager will know his players' strengths and weaknesses and can adjust the formation to suit the forces at his disposal. Others will have their favourite formation and will then try to build a squad of players to fit it. You can tell a lot about a manager's intentions from these numbers, so let's have a closer look at some of them.

Note: Don't worry too much about the numbers on the shirts. These days every player has his own individual squad number, but I thought it would get a bit confusing if I gave you a page of 23, 44, 16 and 5 in midfield with 9 and 32 up front. Prior to 1992, all teams ran out with 1-11 numbers on their back. Ah, they were simpler times.

4-4-2

Nothing says British football like a good old 4-4-2. The most simple and sturdy of the set-ups, it relies upon partnerships all over the pitch. The two full-backs (2 and 3) will attempt to push forward and link up with the two wingers (7 and 11), while the two centre-backs (4 and 5) hold the fort back in their own half. The central midfielders (6 and 8) will try and control the game in the middle, while creating chances for the two strikers (9 and 10).

Everyone knows where they are with 4-4-2, primarily because it tends to be the formation that most people played in at school, but also because of its inherent simplicity. Each player knows precisely where he should be at any period of the game. The classic Liverpool sides of the 1970s and 1980s played 4-4-2, as did the Manchester United teams of the 1990s and if it's good enough for them, it's good enough for anyone.

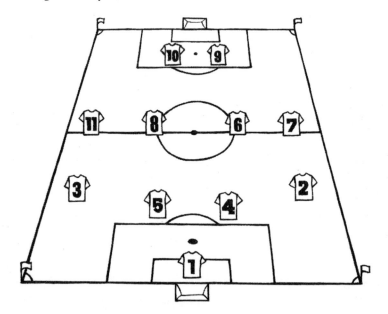

Fig. 2 A typical 4-4-2 formation

However, it has been criticised in the past by those who feel it lacks flexibility and that it is outdated in comparison to some of the more fashionable set-ups. As you'll see, there are other formations that can be changed quickly according to the flow of the game. 4-4-2 doesn't offer that, but it's very, very difficult to screw up and, depending on which team you support, sometimes that's more important than anything else.

Can also be...

It doesn't happen too often these days, but if a 4-4-2 team is losing and the clock is ticking, an adventurous manager can tell his wingers (7 and 11) to push up as extra strikers, making a 4-2-4. Obviously with so many people up front, it leaves huge holes in midfield and it asks a lot of the two remaining midfielders, but that's the price you pay for all-out attack.

4-5-1

This defensive 4-5-1 formation hit the peak of its popularity after 2004 when Greece, the rank outsiders, won the European Championships while using it. It's not popular with neutral observers because it indicates that the manager is more concerned with not losing the game than he is with winning it.

The extra central midfielder (6) sits in front of the defensive line, breaking up the opposition's attempts to create chances. If the other team is playing 4-4-2, it means that the defensive side have an extra man in the middle to dominate the possession of the ball.

Of course, the downside is that there is only one attacker (9) left to fend for himself up front. He'll have to work exceptionally hard to get the ball because he'll be outnumbered

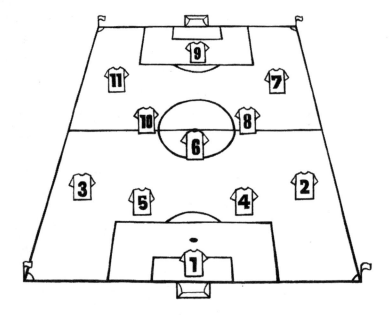

Fig. 3 A typical 4-5-1 formation

by the defenders facing him and he'll have twice as much ground to cover. Mind you, if the other team can't score because of the extra midfielder, he won't need many chances. He just needs one.

Can also be...

If the wingers (7 and 11) move inside behind the attacker (9), the formation becomes a modern 4-3-3. José Mourinho won his first league title at Chelsea in 2005 with this dual formation, pushing Damien Duff and Arjen Robben behind the hard-working Didier Drogba to create a fearsome proposition for any defence. If Chelsea themselves were under pressure, the wingers would simply drop back and return to a 4-5-1. Two for the price of one.

4-2-3-1

This is an interesting formation that seemed more prevalent in international football than in the domestic game, but has gradually seeped into common usage, especially in Europe, where they tend to be a little more sophisticated with their tactics than the English. It offers great flexibility, allowing a team to be very defensive or very offensive, depending on the circumstances.

The two central midfielders (6 and 8) sit in their own half, in front of the defence, providing what their manager would

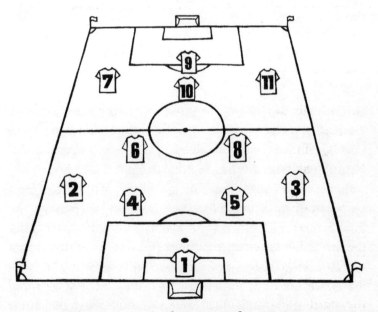

Fig. 4 A typical 4-2-3-1 formation

hope is an impenetrable shield of bodies. Meanwhile, the attacking midfielders (7, 10 and 11) are given the freedom to zip about all over the pitch in search of space. The central attacking midfielder (10) can even move up as a second striker.

Unfortunately, a formation like this requires a lot of practice and great concentration to prevent a large hole opening up in the middle. If the defensive midfielders drop back too far towards their back-line and the attacking midfielders get over-excited, who is left in the centre? It's not a formation to be taken on lightly.

Can also be...

Any team that takes a comfortable lead with this formation can easily put the game out of reach for their opponents by changing to, yep, you've guessed it, 4-5-1. Simply haul the attacking midfielders (7, 10 and 11) back and you've got a nice big wall of players to stop anyone hurting you.

3-5-2

This unorthodox looking set-up was all the rage in the 1990s. Even England gave it a try under former manager Glenn Hoddle, but it never delivered quite as much as it promised.

On a good day, the three central defenders (4, 5 and 6) can stifle any attack that comes their way, especially if the most central of them (5) is deployed as a sweeper (see below). The three central midfielders (7, 8 and 11) can either stretch out towards the wings to find space, or close up into a thick block to outnumber their opponents. Two strikers (9 and 10) give the other manager something to think about if he's not already terrified enough at being outnumbered in almost every critical area of the pitch.

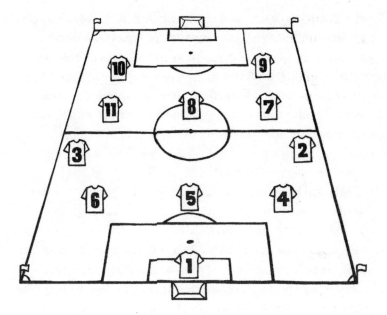

Fig. 5 A typical 3-5-2 formation

Sadly, it suffers from an over-reliance on the attacking full-backs (2 and 3), or wing-backs, as they became known. These poor guys have to defend like full-backs and attack like wingers, essentially playing in two positions at once and spending all afternoon running up and down the flanks. If they're caught out of position, the defenders have to deal with wingers and strikers at the same time and can easily be breached. For most managers, it's too much of a risk to consider.

Can also be...
There isn't an awful lot of versatility in a formation like this, but the wing-backs (2 and 3) can become orthodox full-backs

by dropping back and creating a 5-3-2 that's low on excitement, but very good at withholding pressure.

Specialist positions

There are a couple of positions that have become so well used that they have their own names, and it's always worth learning them to avoid embarrassment.

Sweeper

This is the name given to a defender who provides a kind of auxiliary service to his team, operating on his own as he sees fit. The sweeper, known in Italy as a 'libero', meaning 'free', sits behind the defenders, acting as a last line of defence or even pushing in front of them to distribute the ball to the midfield. He will have no marking responsibilities, just an open remit to stop trouble. See (5) in 3-5-2.

Holding midfielder

This is more commonly known as the 'Makélélé Role' after the success of the former Chelsea and Real Madrid player Claude Makélélé. The holding midfielder is not expected to do anything fancy, he is only there to stop the other team playing football. Usually this will involve snapping at people's heels like a ravenous guard dog, winning the ball only to immediately give it to someone much more talented. See (6) in 4-5-1.

Support striker

Some attackers tend to drop off and sit behind their strike-partner, which can be a lot more dangerous than it sounds. For starters, it means that one of the opposing centre-backs has to decide whether or not to follow him. If they do, they leave a gap in the defence. If they don't, the support striker will have lots of time on the ball. This is what they mean by 'playing in the hole', just in case you've ever heard that expression and wondered what on earth it could refer to. See (10) in 4-2-3-1.

Other formations

Because there is no restriction on the way that players can be deployed, there have been all sorts of wonderful formations in the history of football. In the pre-war years, and for a time afterwards, almost every team used to play a cavalier 2-3-5, which is why you see so many enormous scores in the record books. At the other extreme, some teams can be so afraid of conceding goals that they will line up with no attackers at all, in a 4-6-0, though this is much less entertaining.

There is a school of thought nowadays that formations are redundant. So many teams alter their line-ups as the game progresses, sometimes depending on whether or not they have the ball, that it's too difficult to keep track. Nevertheless, it remains a vital way of understanding how the game is played and the intentions of the teams involved.

Passing

Not even the greatest footballers in the world can win a game on their own. There are ten outfield players on a team and, if that team wants to be successful, they all need to be able to pass a football. But how to do it most effectively? As with all tactics, there's very rarely a right answer, but here's some of the options.

Short passing

It is generally agreed that the most attractive way to play football is to ping the ball around the team as if you're on a sponsored 50p a pass extravaganza. The theory being that if you only ever play a simple ball to the person nearest to you, how are the opposition ever going to get it? And, as we've already established, if the opposition haven't got the ball, they can't score.

Legend has it that Eric Cantona, the mercurial French forward, once took a training session at Manchester United. He asked for one goalkeeper and four defenders and lined them up in a compact formation, making it as difficult as possible for his own small team of attackers to make room for a shot. He then ordered his team to pass the ball between themselves and categorically refused to allow them to have a shot. The whistle blew and his players followed orders, passing the ball left and right across the pitch, always waiting for the defender to come running towards them before knocking the ball to their team-mate. After about a minute of making precisely no progress, one of the attackers shouted, 'Eric, what's going on? We've hardly moved!' Cantona blew his whistle and told everyone to stop still where they were.

'Non,' he said and pointed at the defenders who were now scattered all over the place, panting for breath. 'But they have.'

Short passing may take more time, but it can reduce even the tightest defence to an over-stretched, exhausted line, riddled with nice, exploitable gaps.

Of course, it's not without its problems. Only a skilful, talented team can get away with passing the ball around the pitch without making a mistake and scuffing it towards their opponents, especially if the other team is chasing around after them and crashing into tackles. One false move, one under-hit pass and you'll end up looking very silly indeed.

Long passing

For teams with less skill and more height, long passing may be the best way to go. It's quick and simple and sometimes it can be very effective. After all, no one can run faster than a football if that football is wellied by someone with a foot like a traction engine. Why waste your time playing pretty little passes about in the middle of the pitch when you can just blast it up to the danger zone?

There are two main varieties of long pass. The first is to 'play it up to the big man', which requires the attacker to be very big, very strong and very good at heading the ball. He also needs to be able to keep the ball under control without losing it while the rest of his team scamper forwards to help out. This is known as 'holding the ball up'. Because the striker is so tall, he has a good chance of winning the ball in the air, even if the opposition defenders are jumping up with him.

The other way is to 'play it into the channels', a mysterious footballing term that basically means punting the ball into the zones between the midfield and the defence, at the sides of the pitch. Like a terrier chasing a Frisbee, the quick strikers dart off after it, often with their tongues hanging from their mouths and one of their ears turning inside-out.

The long-ball game is not popular with the fans because it's so desperately boring to watch. As you can imagine, it's a lot harder to pass to someone 40 yards away and the majority of long balls either sail helplessly out of play or are swept up by the defenders. The late Brian Clough, a legendary football manager who you will find out more about later, hated the long-ball game and practically declared war on the FA's Head of Coaching, Charles Hughes, who was a devotee of it.

'Hughes preached a theory that the quicker you could shift the ball from A to B,' Clough wrote in his autobiography of 1993, 'the more likely you would be to score a goal. It was a theory that encouraged a primitive, so-called 'long-ball' game, based on percentages – one that I regard as absolute garbage.'

Of course, it's not a straight choice between one style and the other. Most teams just blend the two together according to the circumstances, but you will notice that some sides are dismissed or lauded according to the style that they are perceived to use. A long cross-field ball is considered more sophisticated than an almighty punt down the centre.

Tempo

If you're listening to the commentary of a football match you will often hear the pundits referring to the 'tempo' of the game. Soundbites like 'They need to up the tempo now, Clive,' or, 'Liverpool are slowing it down now,' are absolutely baffling to the newcomer, but yet another way of understanding how a football team is operating.

A high tempo means that the team in question is frantically knocking the ball around the pitch, often without even taking a touch to bring it under control. One or two-touch football, passing the ball instantly or after only one controlling touch, is tremendously exciting to watch for the dual enjoyment of seeing exemplary technique and also because you know that sooner or later someone is going to slip up and give the ball away. When a team is 'upping the tempo', it means that they will career around the pitch like runaway dodgem cars, trying to do a night's work in 10 minutes. It means fouls, passes, shots and lots of players bent over on their haunches desperately trying to get their breath back. We like a high tempo.

Some teams prefer to play at a slow tempo, gently passing the ball around, taking a few touches, sidestepping a challenge and then knocking the ball back to a defender. It's much easier to play a short-passing game when you're in a languid mood because there is time to enjoy possession and think about what you're going to do with it. There's not much danger of anything exciting happening at a slow tempo, but if you're 2-0 up with ten minutes to go, who cares?

Defending and marking

Defences, like armies, work best when well drilled and working as a unit. No war has ever been won by 500 individuals running round of their own freewill. Even the Vikings had a game plan. Admittedly it was 'hit the monks, grab the shiny stuff', but, you know, it still counts. Most professional football teams are a little more sophisticated than that, although not by much in some cases, and they have detailed instructions every time they take to the field.

Marking is an issue that crops up repeatedly these days. It used to be very simple. Every member of the team would have a man to mark. If the ball was in play and in the possession of your opponents, you would generally mark the person opposite you. For the central defenders, it would tend to be the strikers; for the left-back, it would be the right-winger, and so on and so forth. If it was a set-piece, everyone would know who to stick to and, more pertinently, who to blame if the ball went into the net.

But there were flaws. Imagine that you're a centre-back, charged with marking one of the opposition's two strikers. If, as his team mounts an attack, he runs off in the direction of the corner flag, where are you going to go? That's right, you'll go with him because you're dedicated and you follow your manager's instructions. What does it leave behind you? A whopping great big gap in the defence. You've just been 'dragged out of position'. Now, on this occasion, you'll probably get away with it because the man most likely to take advantage of the gap is the one that you're scurrying after.

However, what happens if one of the midfielders moves up in his place? Or if the opposing manager secretly tells the man you're marking to swap places with one of the wingers? Or if they change formation and have three men up front, outnumbering you and your defensive partner? Tricky, isn't it?

To remedy this, European coaches came up with the concept of 'zonal marking'. Out went the over-familiar relationship with the opposition's number 10 and in came a practice that relied upon concentration, composure and good communication. Let's put you back in the centre-back role. You will be tasked with guarding one zone of the pitch. Now it doesn't matter where the attacker goes, he's only your responsibility if he's in your zone. If he suddenly darts off to the right side of the pitch, it's someone else's problem. Zonal marking really comes into its own in set-pieces where, instead of trying to figure out where the ball is going, while trying to keep an eye on your marker and everyone else and where you're running, the defender just calmly watches his zone and springs into action if the ball enters it.

The slightest lapse of concentration can ruin zonal marking in a flash. Players who are new to it, or just a bit thick, occasionally chase the ball around wherever it goes, drawn to it like a moth to a Maglite. That means gaps in the defence. Zonal marking also means that attacking players can have a free run at the ball from a set-piece because they haven't got a defender hanging off the back of their shirt.

That said, man-marking is compromised by the simple fact that all the defenders are following the actions of the attacker. Unless the defender can read minds, the striker is always going to be a split second in front of him.

Critics point out that men score goals, not zones, so why not mark the man? Believers would argue that all goals are scored from zones, so if you keep them covered you will be alright anyway. It's an argument that shows no signs of ending, sadly.

The line of defence

Now, let's go back to that offside rule. You remember how the strikers couldn't be nearer to the goal than the last defender? Well what about if that defender, and the rest of his colleagues, spent most of the game lined up near the centre circle? Exactly. The attackers would be forced all the way back, almost into their own half, in order to avoid being given offside all the time. Not only that, but with the defensive line there, the midfielders in front of them and the attackers at the top, the opposition would be under constant pressure. This is called 'pushing up'.

Pushing up works exceptionally well if the opposition's attackers are a bit slow, but it can blow up in your face like a cheap firework if they've got a turn of pace. Any ball flighted in above the defenders into that huge gap behind them becomes a dangerous chase for possession. If the attackers can beat the defenders to it, and remember that the defenders will be facing the wrong way to begin with, they get a clean shot on goal.

Far better then, you might think, to drop the line of defenders all the way back. That way they can sit on the edge of the penalty area and absorb anything that comes their way. Sure, the attackers will be able to line up much closer to the goal, but what can they do with all those opponents in front of them? This is known as 'dropping deep'. It means that the other team could have Usain Bolt and Roadrunner up front, but they'd never be able to use their speed effectively because the defenders would have time to move over and stand in front of them. However, if the other team has big, powerful strikers who are good at heading the ball, they'll be able to attack crosses and long balls from much closer to the goal. Too close for anyone who likes a quiet life.

Deep defences can work better if the line is compact, rather than stretched out across the pitch. With four men occupying a tighter space on the pitch, there are more obstacles for the attacking team to avoid. Throw a tight five-man midfield in front of the defence and suddenly the other team is looking at nine shirts in their way. The defensive team, in not using the full width of the pitch, would be limited in the way that they could attack, or 'counter-attack' as it's known, but there wouldn't be much coming through their lines.

As you're no doubt beginning to realise, there is no magic tactic. 4-4-2 is not necessarily better than 4-5-1, 4-3-3 or any other combination you'd like to try and they can be used in so many different ways, none of which are any more worthy or effective than others. Football management is all about selecting the most appropriate tactic for the players available.

Ask a load of hulking great lummoxes who can barely touch their toes to pass the ball around delicately and you'll have a team that loses more than it wins. Get that same team to kick the ball up in the air, push up and then, if robbed of possession, to drop back into tight, compact lines and you'll have Bolton Wanderers. That's one of the many reasons why having a good manager is so important.

5 Why managers are important

Many newcomers to football are baffled by the intense focus on the managers, mainly because it doesn't seem to happen to the same extent in any other sport. How could one person, who isn't even out there on the pitch when the game kicks off, wield so much influence? Short of picking the best players and telling them all to go out and try really, really hard, what can he actually do?

The manager, in the traditional sense at least, is the figurehead of the entire football club. He is the one you will see on the television after every game. He is the one who will sit through press conferences in the lead-up to them. Football fans will form opinions on him and his team purely through what they see in the mass media.

You've just had a brief, believe me I could have been there for hours, introduction to the world of football tactics. The manager's job will depend upon him finding the right blend of them as quickly as possible. Then he'll have to convince his players, many of whom will be experienced highly paid professionals, that he knows what he's talking about. It's not unknown for a squad to consider mutiny at the prospect of a new boss changing the way they play. Not only will he have to know his own team inside out, but he'll also need to know all about his rivals as well because he'll be trying to outsmart them week in, week out, for as long as he remains at the club.

Some managers have very clearly defined and unswerving tactical ideologies. In the 1990s Egil Olsen, an eccentric Norwegian, took his national team from obscurity to a series of international tournaments by playing an uncompromising style of long-ball football. Norway enjoyed great success, against England in particular, by thwacking the ball high into the air and chasing after it in packs. It wasn't very pretty, but that didn't matter. Results were the only thing that Olsen believed in. Unfortunately, when he came to manage Wimbledon, a now defunct English club side, the magic was lost. The players didn't want to play 4-5-1, they didn't understand why the big strikers were being played on the wing and they didn't like the way he mumbled his way through team-talks. Results went awry, Olsen never stood a chance and he left the club shortly before they dropped out of the Premier League forever. One successful team, one successful manager, and yet the chemistry wasn't there and it ended in disaster.

On the flip-side you have Leicester City circa 1995, a fairly average club languishing in the second division and Martin O'Neill, a manager who had just endured an unhappy time at Norwich City and whose main achievement was taking Wycombe Wanderers out of non-league and into the fourth division. O'Neill inspired his players to perform above themselves. He brought in undiscovered gems from obscurity, he got the best out of wayward talents. Leicester were promoted to the Premier League, never finished outside the top half under his control and even qualified for Europe when they won the League Cup. One mediocre team, one relatively untested manager, and it became one of the success stories of the decade.

Real football isn't like the computer games or the management simulations. Footballers are not numbers and there is no easy five-star rating to tell you who the best players are. They are human beings with different skill bases, subject to the same changes in mood and determination as you or I. The most important role of a manager is to judge what his players can and can't do and then to motivate them. Believe it or not, there are players scattered in the lower leagues with just as much natural talent as their Premier League counterparts. For one reason or another they haven't achieved their potential, usually because a manager has failed to motivate or use them correctly, or simply because he hasn't realised how good they really are. Of course, some of them are down there purely because they're rubbish at football, but that's another matter.

Brian 'Killer' Kilcline was never the most gifted of footballers. A towering centre-half with long blond hair and a bushy moustache, he was more Anglo-Saxon warrior than professional athlete. He specialised in crunching tackles and powerful headers, intimidating his opponents with a blatant disregard for his own safety. Bobby Moore he was not. Nevertheless, when Kevin Keegan took over a struggling Newcastle United in 1992, his first move was to splash out on this unreconstructed madman and make him captain of the team. Keegan knew that, with relegation beckoning, his side needed a leader. Kilcline wasn't the greatest player, but you wouldn't argue with him if he told you to run through a plate glass window. With no small amount of shouting, and with fire in their bellies, Newcastle avoided the drop and were promoted to the Premier League the next season. Kilcline was gradually phased out as results improved and eventually allowed to leave the club. His work there was complete.

Not many managers would have taken a chance on Kilcline, but that's why not many managers go more than two or three seasons without being sacked. It takes tactical acumen, an eye for a player, motivational genius, boundless charisma and an ability to deal with pressure to survive in football management. Hardly any managers have all those attributes. Keegan, for example, lacked the last one. Let's have a look at some of the best.

Managers you should know about
Sir Alex Ferguson
There are few sights in football as terrifying as Sir Alex Ferguson in a rage. Manager of Manchester United since 1986 and winner of countless competitions, the fiery Scotsman is as well known for his temper as he is for his talent. It was his hapless players who first coined the phrase 'the hairdryer' as a way of describing his close-range, spittle-flecked rollickings and it's an image that, once it arrives in your mind, stubbornly refuses to ever leave again.

But 'Fergie' offers much more than just tantrums. He is fiercely loyal to his players, an excellent judge of talent, a believer in the power of youth, and yet he is capable of clinical ruthlessness to those he deems to have outstayed their welcome. Not only is he unafraid of the press, but he has given some sections of the press reason to be afraid of him. He is wise enough not to get stuck in his ways and has always been able to spot developing trends in the game before they overwhelm him. He knew in the mid 80s that the 'win or lose, we're on the booze' mentality of English football was hopelessly outdated and, as formations evolved in the early 21st century, he brought the tactical expert Carlos Quieroz back to the club to help design a more fluid deployment of his troops. Enthusiastic and well read, there isn't much that takes him by surprise.

Sir Alex can also claim to have earned his place at the pinnacle of European football. A decent, but undistinguished striker in Scotland, he began his managerial career at East Stirlingshire, an impoverished and unfashionable lower league side. He was well thought of enough to be given a chance at St Mirren where his success brought him to the attention of one of Scotland's larger club sides, Aberdeen. It was here that he really made his name, breaking up the dominance of Glasgow Rangers and Celtic, the Old Firm of Scottish football, and winning a European trophy against Real Madrid to boot.

He was the obvious choice to rejuvenate a Manchester United side that had stagnated since their glory days in the 1960s, but the dominance that you see today was a long time in coming. It wasn't until 1990 that Sir Alex was able to deliver an FA Cup as proof that his long rebuilding project was taking shape. But with that first trophy in the bag a golden age was underway and, even at the time of writing, 23 years on from his arrival, it shows no sign of ending.

Arsène Wenger

'Arsène Who?' was how the *London Evening Standard* welcomed one of the most influential managers to grace English football, and it was a reaction shared by many inside the Arsenal dressing room. Wenger was French, and with his grey suits and spectacles looked more like a geography teacher than a football manager. What on earth could he teach the country that gave football to the world? Quite a lot, it turned out.

Erudite and enthusiastic, he believed that football should be beautiful and not just an ugly means to a necessary end. This was quite a departure for Arsenal, who had spent the 80s and early 90s playing a breed of football that was about as exciting and attractive as partying with the Young Conservatives. 1-0 wins were always the order of the day under previous managers, but Wenger bucked the trend. Away fans used to sing, 'Boring, Boring Arsenal,' whenever they visited Highbury, but all of a sudden it was the home fans who adopted the song as an ironic tribute to their newfound flair.

Wenger was also one of the first managers to insist that his players behave like professional athletes and not old soaks, but he went even further than Sir Alex Ferguson, introducing special dietary plans to get the best out of his squad. In came a host of European talent, most of it undiscovered and unrecognised by everyone else, and an encouraging first season ended in 1997 with a third place finish. The next season delivered a rare double of the league title and the FA Cup. In 2002, Wenger invited ridicule by suggesting that his team could go an entire season without being beaten. In the 2003/4 season, he did it, winning another title in the process.

Like Ferguson, Wenger's achievements as a player were modest. As a manager, he worked his way up from junior football, through to Cannes, then Nancy and then Monaco where he won the French title. A lucrative deal in Japan tempted him to join Grampus 8 in 1994, but Arsenal's vice-chairman David Dein had already noticed his talents and eventually managed to lure him to London. Dein knew, rather better than the local press, that this was a man who could bring his football club kicking and screaming into the 21st century.

Wenger's scouts scour the world for young talent and the club's academy produces a flow of rookies, all indoctrinated in the art of quick, free-flowing football. For a manager to enjoy such success with a team is admirable enough, but to do it by completely overhauling the style and mentality of the entire club is something else.

Brian Clough

Arguably the most fascinating character in the history of football, Brian Clough was a manager of extraordinary talents, but also a man of bewildering contrasts. Capable of acts of great generosity and kindness, he could also be irascible, arrogant and short-tempered. He was entirely unpredictable off the pitch, but phenomenally successful on it and you can say with some confidence that his achievements will never be matched.

Clough was a goalscorer of tremendous proficiency, rattling in goals at the rate of almost one a game, but a knee injury ended his playing career just as he was at his peak. Disastrous as it was, for in those days of modest wages a serious injury was exactly that, it drove Clough on and made his success in management even more likely.

Pick a team at the bottom of the Championship. Any team. Now imagine them rising up the table and being promoted. Now see them winning the Premier League in their first season up. Now they're in the semi-finals of the Champions League. Ok, now he's been sacked. Pick another team at the bottom of the second flight. Imagine them going up. Imagine them winning the league. Imagine them winning the Champions League. Twice. That was Clough.

Of course, his career wasn't an unbroken success. It couldn't be with his personality. His 44-day stint at Leeds United in 1974 was an unmitigated disaster, not helped by his opening speech to the players in which he asked them to throw away all their medals because they'd won them all by cheating. It wasn't much better at Brighton either, where his gift for motivation utterly failed to ignite a struggling club.

But at Derby County, the first of his success stories, everything fell into place. He somehow managed to talk Dave McKay, the Tottenham legend, into dropping down a division and then built an exciting young team around him. Silverware followed, but so too did a furious row with the chairman Sam Longson, and Clough left the club. After the disappointments of Leeds and Brighton, he ended up at Nottingham Forest, where he quickly repeated the success of Derby, adding two European Cups as well, in 1979 and 1980.

Unfortunately, he stayed on too long. Forest continued to win the occasional League Cup, but by the end they were no longer in contention for the title. His relationship with assistant manager Peter Taylor, a man whose talents were key to Clough's success, collapsed and his drinking began to creep out of control. In his final season, 1992/3, his touch deserted him completely and Forest were relegated from the Premier League. He remains a cult hero to English football fans and, understandably, an immortal in the towns of Derby and Nottingham.

Bill Shankly

Today, Liverpool are a global brand with fans in every corner of the planet. In 1959, they were just another under-achieving second flight outfit with very little to differentiate them from any other team in the north-west. Shankly gave them their soul. Not only did he rebuild the entire club on the solid, sensible foundations of 'pass and move', but he understood what a football team's purpose was in the community. It wasn't there to make money, it was there to give the people something to believe in.

The timing was perfect. The city of Liverpool boomed in the 1960s, partly because of The Beatles, partly because of the football. In 1963/4, Shankly's team snatched the title away from their local rivals Everton and started to establish themselves as the dominant force in English football. European trophies and FA Cups followed, but the silverware never dented Shankly's sense of priorities. 'The league,' he once said, 'is our bread and butter.'

Quotes were Shankly's stock in trade. He wanted Anfield to become a 'bastion of invincibility'. He refused to overcomplicate matters, telling his players, 'If you're not sure what to do, pop the ball in the net and we'll discuss your options afterwards.' Most famously of all, he once told reporters, 'Some people believe football is a matter of life and death. I'm very disappointed with that attitude. I can assure you, it is much, much more important than that.'

This, though, was more of a wisecrack than an ideology. As important as football was to him, he often seemed more concerned with the way the players handled themselves and the way that the club was represented. Stories of him buying tickets for impoverished fans are legion, as are the accounts of him chastising players who failed to sign autographs. 'At a football club,' he said, 'there is a holy trinity. The players, the manager and the supporters.'

When he suddenly retired in 1974, the city went into a state of shock. Factories threatened to launch wildcat strikes if he didn't return. Shankly was adamant though. At the age of 60, he wanted to spend more time with his wife and family. He died in 1981 of a heart attack and, at the first home game after his funeral, the Liverpool fans unfurled a banner that said it all: 'Shankly Lives Forever.'

Sir Matt Busby

Just as Bill Shankly will forever be synonymous with Liverpool, Manchester United will always belong to Sir Matt Busby, the dignified and wise manager who led the club to their greatest triumph, but more importantly, held it together in its bleakest hour.

Busby was appointed as Manchester United manager in 1945 and, from the first post-war season of 1946/7, led the team to second place in four years out of the next five, finally winning the title in 1951. Then, with age catching up with his squad, he built another team – even better than his first – and they won back-to-back titles in 1956 and 1957. Busby's willingness to field young talent, especially the supremely gifted Duncan Edwards, earned his team the nickname, 'The Busby Babes'.

The Babes could have been one of the greatest teams of all time, but tragedy struck on the night of 6 February 1958, when their plane crashed on takeoff at Munich airport. Seven Manchester United players, including Edwards, were among the 23 dead. Busby's injuries were so severe that he was administered with the last rites on two separate occasions, before eventually recovering in time for the FA Cup Final that his assistant manager's makeshift team of reserves and youth players had somehow reached. United were beaten by Bolton and Busby predicted that it would take five years to rebuild them.

He was absolutely right. In 1963, United were back in the FA Cup Final, but this time they were the winners at Wembley. The season after that brought a runners-up spot in the league, but they lifted the title in 1965 and then again in 1967. But while that was more than enough to secure Busby's legendary status, the best was yet to come.

Busby had always said that the European Cup, the competition that United had been returning from on that wintry night in 1958, was the future of football and that English teams should embrace it rather than avoid it, as they had in the past. Ten years later, in an emotional night at Wembley, his rejuvenated, rebuilt team, with youngsters like George Best and veteran survivors of the crash like Bobby Charlton, beat Benfica 4-1 in the final. 'We won this for Matt, and for all the boys who died in Munich,' said Bill Foulkes, another surviving player, at the time. Busby, who had captured the hearts of football fans across the country, was subsequently knighted and he retired a year later.

After a brief spell returning as caretaker manager, Busby joined the board of directors and eventually became the president of the football club. He died in 1994, but his ethos lives on in the present-day Manchester United team.

'There is nothing wrong with trying to win,' he told an audience after being made a Freeman of Manchester, 'so long as you don't set the prize above the game. There is no dishonour in defeat, so long as you play to the limit of your strength and skill.'

Sir Alf Ramsey

The man responsible for England's greatest footballing moment was also present for her most grievous humiliation. Alf Ramsey, an intelligent but ponderous right-back, was once asked by a reporter if he had played in the infamous 0-1 defeat by the United States in 1950. 'I was the only one who did,' he responded typically.

It was this steely self-belief and single-mindedness that enabled him to progress so far in football management, especially as his most famous triumph, the World Cup win of 1966, came in the face of a stream of criticism from the media, an industry he never hid his disdain from.

'I have to make a living just like you,' he told them once. 'I happen to make mine in a nice way whereas you make yours in a nasty way.'

His 'nice way' was to guide lowly Ipswich Town from the third division all the way to the top flight, winning the title in 1962. His success made him an obvious choice to succeed Walter Winterbottom as the national team manager.

Ramsey had to be strong. His decision to drop wingers and play a narrow midfield was widely derided and when he left Jimmy Greaves, one of the most natural and prolific English goalscorers of all time, out of the team, the criticism intensified.

But Ramsey was vindicated by the players that he did pick, especially Nobby Stiles. A crunching tackle by the Manchester United player infuriated the Football Association, who wanted to drop him from the squad. Ramsey refused and defended his player to the hilt, ignoring the barbs in the newspapers.

On 30 July 1966, England met West Germany in the World Cup Final at Wembley. The Germans opened the scoring, only to be pegged back quickly by a Geoff Hurst equaliser. England looked to have won the game with 12 minutes remaining when Martin Peters scored, but their hearts were broken by a last-minute German strike from Wolfgang Weber. Now Ramsey had to lift his players for extra time. 'You've won it once,' he told them. 'Now go out and win it again.' Hurst then crashed one in off the crossbar which our generous Azerbaijani linesman friend was happy to award, before rocketing home his third, right on full-time to make it 4-2.

After the match a journalist said to Ramsey, 'We've done it, Alf! We've won the World Cup!'

'We?' growled Ramsey. 'What do you mean *we*?'

6

The competitions

Domestic
The English Leagues

There are 92 professional football teams in England divided into four divisions. A long time ago, when sanity reigned over the game, the best teams played in the first division, the worst in the fourth division. It was nice, simple and easy for newcomers to understand. However, after the schism of the early 90s and the creation of the Premier League, it became a little more complicated. Now the Premier League was the top division, and the second division became the first division, the third the second and the fourth the third. Easy, eh? Ah, but wait. In 2004, in a much-mocked effort to 'rebrand' and 'strengthen identities', the Football League decided to mess with the system once again. Apparently, the name 'first division' wasn't catchy enough to reflect the new found hubris of the second flight. The Championship though, that's much better! Mind you, it did leave a gap in the market for a division with a one in the title and it was eagerly exploited by the old third division which became, with no sense of either irony or shame, League One. And, yes, you've guessed it. The old fourth division became League Two. So to clarify:

Premier League (20 teams)
Championship (24 teams)
League One (24 teams)
League Two (24 teams)

Over the course of a league season, every team within each of the divisions plays each other twice. Once at their stadium, once at their opponents'. In a 90-minute game, the teams are awarded three points for a win, they each receive one point for a draw and the losers go away empty-handed. After every single match a 'league table' is updated in order of the teams with the most points. If two teams are on identical points, they are separated by goal difference, which is the difference between the amount of goals a team have scored and the amount they have conceded. Obviously any team keen on winning something will have a goal difference in positive figures. It gets very depressing to see a minus figure there on the league table.

At the end of the football season, when all the fixtures have been completed, you will have the final league table. And this is where it gets interesting.

Promotion and relegation

English football is in a constant state of meritocratic flux. For there to be any point to the whole system, the good must be rewarded and the unworthy punished. The team at the top of the Premier League will earn the right to call themselves champions, rulers of all they survey. The three teams at the bottom will be flushed away and 'relegated' from this league. They will be replaced by three teams promoted from the Championship. This is promotion and relegation.

Down in the Championship, 24 teams will have been slogging away and at the end of the season the top two will be promoted to the Premier League. The four teams behind them will then battle it out in the 'play-offs' to decide the identity of the third promotees. The team in third place will play the team in sixth twice, once at their ground (home), once at their opponents' (away). When the two scores are combined, the winner on 'aggregate', that is the total score combined (but more on that later), will go through to a final against the winner of the battle between fourth and fifth.

The Championship Play-Off Final is often the most exciting match of the football season because there's so much riding on it. Each team will have played 48 games over ten months and their future will be decided on the outcome of one match. Because of the vast financial rewards on offer in the Premier League, it is often referred to in the press as the £30m game, or the £40m game, depending on how many cans of sugary pop the journalist in question has consumed.

Down at the bottom of the Championship, three more teams will be sucked down and replaced by the top two in League One, as well as the winner of their play-off. In League One, four unfortunate teams will suffer the indignity of relegation, swapping places with the top three in League Two, and the winners of that play-off final as well.

The saddest sight is always the relegation zone of League Two where a pair of sorry, misbegotten teams will wave farewell to the Football League, replaced Doctor Who-style by a couple of chancers from non-league.

Non-league football is a different animal entirely and would take many more pages than the publishers have given me to explain and illustrate. Suffice to say that there is another league down beneath the bedrock, a subterranean fifth division commonly known as 'the Conference' and fed by two tributary regional leagues that make up the tip of the non-league pyramid.

Whatever else happens in football, whatever other competitions are entered and won or lost, every club is defined by how they perform in the league. Some have been languishing in League Two for generations; others like to take whistle-stop tours up and down the divisions, stopping in to pay a visit to the big boys before relegation drags them away again. Bradford City, for example, were relegated from the Premier League in 2001, the Championship in 2004 and League One in 2007. Maybe one day they'll be back. In football, you can't rule out anything.

Scottish League

The set-up of Scottish football is very similar to the English game, but on a smaller scale. There are still four divisions, but with considerably fewer members than their English counterparts. They've also thrown in a few twists and turns to keep things interesting.

Scottish Premier League (12 teams)
First Division (10 teams)
Second Division (10 teams)
Third Division (10 teams)

Now, hang on to your hats, because the Scottish FA apparently thought the old system of promotion and relegation was far too straightforward, so they've got their own ideas.

All Scottish Premier League (SPL) teams play each other three times. Yep, once away and twice at home or vice versa. After 33 matches, the league table is split into two sections. The six teams at the top then complete their fixtures against each other, leaving the bottom six to scrap it out amongst themselves. It sounds absolutely bonkers, but there are two key benefits. Firstly, it means that teams play 38 games in a season and not a more strenuous 44. Secondly, it increases the chances of some rip-roaring fixtures towards the end of the campaign.

It does have a few drawbacks though. Because of the relative ease of the fixtures in the bottom section, it's not unknown for the team in seventh to end up with more points than the team in sixth, or even in fifth. It can also weaken the integrity of the league a little, especially if some teams get two nice and easy home games against the weakest side in the division, while their major rivals have to go and play that same small side twice, but away from home. To that end, the Scottish FA seed the teams at the beginning of the league season and try to arrange the fixtures accordingly.

The team at the bottom of the SPL is relegated into the First Division and replaced by the team who have just won it. At the bottom of the First Division, the last-placed team are relegated into the Second Division while the team in ninth are forced into play-offs against that division's second, third and fourth placed sides. The same thing happens with the teams at the bottom of the Second Division, who clash with the Third Division's chasing pack, and there is no relegation from the bottom of the basement. Got all that? Excellent!

The FA Cup

The English FA Cup is the most famous club competition in the world, mainly because it's the oldest, but also because of its beautiful simplicity. It is open to football clubs all over the country, both professional and amateur. The 2009/10 competition accepted 762 teams, from Arsenal to Yaxley. (No, I don't know where Yaxley is either.)

The little teams will start the process at the beginning of the season, fighting among themselves through a number of preliminary rounds until just 32 remain. They are then thrown into the pot with the 48 teams from League One and League Two and drawn out of a hat at random for the FA Cup first round.

The 40 who progress from that will then be drawn out, again at random, for the second round. With just 20 remaining, the 20 Premier League teams and the 24 Championship teams are brought in for the third round draw which, for some fans, can be the most wonderful moment of the season.

Aside from the staggered start, there is no seeding in the FA Cup whatsoever. This means that dear old Yaxley (I've just looked them up, they're from near Peterborough and they play in something called the Eagle Bitter United Counties Football League) could scrap their way past the likes of St Ives and Braintree, push past Welling or Northwich Victoria, fluke a win over Rochdale, skim past Colchester and then find themselves with a trip to Old Trafford and a glamour tie against Manchester United. The wonderfully named Ricky Hailstone (I've been on their website, nasty colour scheme, but very informative) would be out there for Yaxley, up against international defenders and watched by millions on television.

Astonishingly, this kind of thing happens quite a lot in the FA Cup and if the smaller team should ever win, it's called a 'giant-killing'. Non-league Hereford once knocked out Newcastle with a wonder goal from Ronnie Radford. Part-timers Sutton disposed of top-flight and former cup holders Coventry City in 1989. Non-league wins over big teams are rare these days, but as recently as 2008, Liverpool found themselves trailing to little Havant & Waterlooville twice before eventually winning 5-2.

If two teams draw their game at any stage of the competition aside from the final itself, a replay is held at the away team's ground. If this is a draw as well, the match moves to extra time and penalties, which we'll look at in more detail later. The important thing to know is that from the 64 teams that are drawn for the third round, only 32 will go to the fourth round. A fifth round of 16 is followed by a sixth round of 8, commonly known as the 'quarter-finals' and then you have the semi-finals and the final itself.

The FA Cup Final is the showpiece event of the football season. Tickets go out to every local football association and millions tune in to it on TVs around the world. The FA Cup used to be almost as important as winning the league, but its relevance has sagged a little in recent years. The astonishing amount of money on offer in the Premier League means that a few clubs have started to field weakened sides, saving themselves for the challenge of staying in the top flight. In the old days, an eliminated team could say that their defeat gave them a chance to 'concentrate on the league.' Now all too many of them say that they'd like to do that before the game has even kicked off.

To understand the love for the FA Cup, you have to realise that for decades it was one of the few televised games of the season and, because of that, it's often the first football match that people ever watched. The build-up was extraordinary, sometimes starting hours before the game even kicked off, with footage of the team coach arriving, profiles of the players and endless analysis in the studio. Of course, you get that build-up for every game now, another reason that the old cup has lost its shine.

Scottish Cup

The Scottish FA Cup is the oldest football trophy in the world. The English FA Cup competition may have been running for longer, but the Scottish Cup was the first to be cast. The competition itself is very similar to its English counterpart in that it is a straight, unseeded tournament with teams drawn out of the hat at random, playing one replay if necessary that ends with extra time and penalties if the deadlock still cannot be broken.

The first round sees a mixture of junior league clubs and semi-professional outfits like Bruntisland Shipyard and the Civil Service Strollers going to battle. The Scottish definitely have a monopoly on the best team names, by the way. The surviving 18 meet up with four more semi-pro sides and the teams from the Third Division to make up a 32-team second round.

The 16 winners of that then go into the third round with the bottom six of the First Division and all of the Second Division, before the SPL teams join the fray for the fourth round. See? Simple.

The English League Cup

The League Cup is open to all 92 clubs, but not to the non-league sides. Something of a poor relation to the FA Cup, it began in 1961 and has been known under various guises since it became the Milk Cup in 1982, including the Coca-Cola Cup, the Carling Cup and my personal favourite, the Rumbelows Cup.

The competition enjoyed something of a heyday in the 1980s when English teams were banned from playing in Europe and had a bit more time on their hands, but when the big boys were allowed abroad again, the appeal of this secondary competition died off. Many teams use it as a chance to test out their youngsters or to give their reserves a run-out, which is why you often see a number of less fashionable sides in the later stages.

Not that this is a bad thing of course. Football gets very boring when the same teams win all the time and the League Cup has produced some magnificent matches. The lower league clubs contest the first round in single games decided by extra time and penalties if necessary. The bulk of the Premier League teams join the fray for the second round and in the third round, the teams who have qualified for Europe are invited along. The semi-finals are two-legged affairs, home and away, and by that stage, even if a team wasn't taking it seriously in the first place, the prospect of a trip to Wembley and some silverware usually makes them think again.

Scottish League Cup and Scottish Challenge Cup

The Scottish League Cup is open only to the 42 Scottish League teams and again, like its equivalent in England, it is staggered to accommodate the congested diaries of the clubs in Europe. The lower leagues open the tournament, with the bulk of the SPL joining in the second round and the four Scottish European qualifiers arriving in time for the third. The games are straight knockout affairs with no replays, using extra time and penalties to determine a winner on the night.

The Scottish Challenge Cup is a competition open only to the teams outside of the SPL. It is concluded quickly, with the final usually played before December, and it gives teams outside of the elite a chance for silverware and recognition. As such, I'm afraid that it is widely ignored by the media.

European
The UEFA Champions League and the Europa League

The best teams in Europe win the right to compete against each other in the UEFA Champions League, a glossy, cash-rich competition that replaced the European Cup in 1992. The original idea of this competition, as the name suggests, was to give every nation's champion a chance to fight it out for the cup, but gradually that has given way to the entrance of the top two, the top three and in England's case, the qualification of the top four in the division. This gives the competition a greater pool of big-name teams, but also leads to rather bizarre anomalies like Liverpool's 2005 Champions League victory, which came 15 years after they were last named champions of England. Mind you, the money that surges into UEFA's coffers through widespread sponsorship and earth-shattering TV deals is more than enough to make up for that. In any case, UEFA make sure that the teams who finish second, as well as the champions of the big leagues like England, Spain and Italy qualify automatically for the group stage.

Like the FA Cup, the competition begins in the summer with a frantic battle between the minnows as they scrap through three two-legged preliminary rounds. Unlike the FA Cup, the draws are carefully seeded in order to guard against the possibility of an unfashionable and therefore unmarketable side sneaking into the lucrative group stages. That said, UEFA did make changes to the qualification process in 2009 to ensure an easier ride for actual champions, forcing some of the less successful big names to fight it out in their own fenced-off half of the final preliminary round.

Then, with no small amount of fanfare, the 16 preliminary qualifiers will meet up with the 16 automatic qualifiers and be drawn out into eight groups of four. This is the Champions League group stage and any team that gets this far will make millions and millions of pounds in television revenue, not to mention all the extra ticket money they get from those extra games. The four teams play each other twice, home and away, with the top two in the group going through to the knockout round. Those groups are, yes, you've guessed it, seeded. There will be the occasional group with some good matches, but you can usually look at the draw and safely predict the identity of the majority of the eventual qualifiers.

After all that, the last sixteen finally move into a knockout competition and this is where the Champions League finally bursts into life. There is nothing quite like watching the best teams in Europe going up against each other and there have been some truly awesome battles in recent years.

Let's look a bit closer at the concept of home and away games. We've already covered the fact that they are decided by 'aggregate scores', but what happens if those scores are level? If Liverpool draw 1-1 at home to Barcelona and then 2-2 away, the aggregate score is 3-3. Who goes through?

This is where 'away goals' come in. As you can imagine, it's generally easier for a player to play well at home than it is away. You don't have to travel so far, you're comfortable in your surroundings, the vast majority of the people in the stadium love you and, rather than having to zip off to the airport straight after the game, you know you can go straight home instead. Much nicer. With that in mind, many competitions use the amount of away goals as a sort of tie-breaker. In the example above, Liverpool would go through because they scored twice in Spain, while Barcelona only scored once in England.

Away goals are a lifeline for any team that take a beating in the first leg of their game. For example, if Manchester United went to AC Milan and lost 3-1, it would be bad, but it wouldn't be a disaster. That single goal in Italy would mean that just a 2-0 win back at Old Trafford would see them through. The aggregate score would be 3-3, but United would win on away goals because they scored in Italy and AC Milan didn't score in England.

The same system works with the Europa League, formerly known as the UEFA Cup. This is a competition for the teams that didn't qualify for the Champions League, or who were knocked out in the early stages. Unfortunately, as UEFA change the format of the competition with such regularity, there's very little point in discussing it much further.

Back in the UEFA Champions League, the knockout stages continue until the final, held in a pre-determined stadium, which everyone hopes is neutral. It doesn't always work out like that. For example, Liverpool made it all the way to the final in 1984 to face the mighty AS Roma, a difficult enough adversary at the best of times, but even more tricky given that the final was held in ... erm ... Rome. The Merseysiders won that game after extra time and penalties and it's probably a good time to take a look at those dramatic phases of the game.

Extra time

If two teams can't be separated over the course of the two legs, even by away goals, then the match moves to extra time. This is also the case in the FA Cup, after full-time in a replay, and in the League Cup, after full-time. The referee will give the players a couple of minutes to get their breath back, the two teams swap ends and then the game begins again for a 15-minute half. Regardless of the score at the end of that period, the referee will blow his whistle, the two teams will swap ends again and then play out a final 15-minute period.

Extra time is now always 30 minutes and it doesn't matter what happens, that time has to be played out. The football authorities did experiment with 'Golden Goals' where the first team to score won the game, but they found that players were so haunted by the prospect of losing the game that no one bothered to attack, so it was scrapped. There was also a 'Silver Goal' where if one team was leading halfway through extra time, they won the game, but that too was scrapped because it was all getting a little too complicated.

Even without golden and silver goals, it can still be very difficult to tempt teams to attack. Some, like Liverpool and Roma in 1984, are quite happy to bide their time and wait for the penalty shoot-out. Let's have a look at that.

Penalty shoot-out

When two teams just can't be separated, the referee will call for penalties to decide the eventual winner. The two managers will wander around their players, asking for brave volunteers and then pass a list of designated and ordered penalty takers, five from each team, to the officials. Then the blow-by-blow finale will begin and the two teams will take turns until victory is certain. Let's use that Liverpool-Roma game as an example.

Liverpool had the honour of stepping up first, but it didn't help them at all. Young Steve Nicol blasted the ball high over the bar. Not a good start. (Liv 0-0 Rom)

Agostino Di Bartolomei had a chance to give his team the advantage and he took it well, slotting it past Bruce Grobbelaar (Liv 0-1 Rom)

Now Phil Neal was in a bit of a sticky situation because if he missed, the Italians would go two goals up. He didn't though. (Liv 1-1 Rom)

Bruno Conti, the wonderfully talented Roma midfielder, was next, but the pressure got to him and he missed the goal completely. All square after two penalties each. (Liv 1-1 Rom)

Graeme Souness, the Liverpool captain, was an aggressive, fiery character and it showed with his penalty, a rocket into the top corner. (Liv 2-1 Rom)

Ubaldo Righetti used an old trick to score his penalty: he looked at one side of the goal and sent the ball screaming into the other. (Liv 2-2 Rom)

Ian Rush was one of the finest strikers that Liverpool ever had and he slid the team's fourth penalty into the bottom corner, the hardest place for a goalkeeper to reach. (Liv 3-2 Rom)

Francesco Graziani couldn't afford to miss Roma's fourth spot kick, but Bruce Grobbelaar started wobbling about on the goal-line and the Italian was put off. He hit the bar. (Liv 3-2 Rom)

Now it was Alan Kennedy's turn and because it was the final round of penalties, he knew that he could win the European Cup for Liverpool if he scored because Roma only had one kick left and they would be 4-2 down. He put the ball on the spot, took a short run-up and slammed the ball straight down the middle as the goalkeeper dived off to the side. (Liv 4-2 Rom)

Unlike normal penalties, the shoot-out is a simple hit-or-miss affair. If the ball cannons off the post or the bar, it can't be touched. If the goalkeeper palms it back to the penalty taker, he can't have another go and slam it past his ears.

So, as you can see, missing your first penalty doesn't matter as much as you might think. It's the total score after all the penalties that counts, assuming that the result hasn't already been decided. Even the football authorities wouldn't be cruel enough to make players take unnecessary spot kicks when the other team is already dancing around celebrating.

If the two teams, for example, score all of their penalties and draw 5-5, the shoot-out goes into 'sudden death'. The managers now have to select players who didn't want to take a normal penalty and ask them to take a much more important one. If the stalemate continues, even the goalkeepers will have to have a go. However, given the incredible pressure on the individuals concerned, sudden death tends to be over very quickly. Of course, if it does go to 11-11, or whatever combination of hits and misses leads to stalemate, the sudden death continues, and those players slumped on the floor thanking their stars that it's all over? They'll have to step up and take another one. It is quite possible for a man to miss two penalties in one shoot-out.

If you're a neutral, penalties are hilarious. Two teams forced into a battle of nerves until one luckless player misses and has to relive the moment in his nightmares for the rest of his life. You tell me where you can find comedy like that anywhere else. For a fan, it's absolute hell. How can one game be decided on a test of nerve? It's a rotten end to a match and it's cruel on the players. Penalties, you see, are all about perspective.

International

Running alongside the domestic game and the European competitions is international football, generally regarded as being the highest level of the game. International managers are employed to pick the best players from their respective nations and to compete for regional trophies, like the European Championships, and for the World Cup, the biggest prize in football.

The World Cup is held every four years and most nations spend more than a year just trying to qualify for it. They'll be drawn into seeded groups, usually with six or seven other nations, and made to play home and away, with the best progressing to the actual tournament, which is always held in the summer in a country chosen by FIFA several years beforehand.

At the tournament itself, 32 nations are drawn into eight groups with the top two qualifying for a pre-determined knockout stage. Extra time and penalties, combined with the knowledge that millions of people around the world watch every game, make these games some of the most exciting and nerve-wracking you will ever see.

World Cups are the best time to be into football; in fact, along with FA Cup Finals, it's where a lot of people first fall in love with the game. You get months of speculation in the build-up, huge magazine pullouts, pre-tournament guides, and then it all kicks off with games coming at you at the rate of two or three a day. This is why pubs are crammed on random summer afternoons, why people sneak radios into the office and why you may have heard men and women rattling away at the bus stop about the Ecuadorean threat. It should all make sense now.

International management isn't easy, despite what people seem to think. There is the pressure of picking a team that the entire nation will probably disagree with, the difficulty of coming up against teams from around the world, many of whom will be unfamiliar, and then there's the problem of bringing together a competitive side using players from different clubs. If you believe what you read in the newspapers, the England squad was once split because the Liverpool players were alleged to be avoiding the Manchester United players.

In the even-numbered year between World Cups, you will always find the European Championships, very similar to the World Cup, but with obvious geographical limitations to the competitors and on a slightly smaller scale. Other continents have their own tournaments, like the Copa America and the African Nations Cup, so there's a lot going on throughout the year. This is why footballers often moan about being tired, you see.

Players you should know about

Pelé

Pelé is widely regarded as the greatest footballer of all time and for good reason. The Brazilian scored 1,282 goals in 1,363 matches in a career spanning 21 years. He won three World Cups, played almost 100 times for his country and was one of the figureheads for the big money North American Soccer League of the 1970s. Not bad for a poor kid from São Paulo.

Pelé spent the majority of his career at the Brazilian team Santos, making his debut in 1956, just a month before his 16th birthday. Despite his tender years, he was included in the 1958 World Cup squad and proved any doubters wrong by becoming the youngest goalscorer in tournament history when he picked up the only goal of the game in a quarter-final tussle with Wales. A hat-trick in the semi-finals put him on the global map before two more goals in a 5-2 win over Sweden in the final secured his place in World Cup legend. But Pelé had only just begun.

An injury in Brazil's second match ruled him out of the bulk of the 1962 World Cup, but his team went on to win the trophy without him regardless. Pelé was awarded a winners medal in 2007 by FIFA, which was a nice thought, but probably a little late. He was kicked from pillar to post in England in 1966 and left the field black and blue after a battering from Portugal. Brazil crashed out and Pelé pledged never to play in a World Cup again.

Fortunately for football, he was bluffing and he returned four years later as part of the greatest team ever, the Brazil 1970 squad, who swept to glory in Mexico. After Pelé destroyed Italy 4-1 in the final, his marker Tarcisio Burgnich explained to the press, 'I told myself before the game that he's made of skin and bones just like everyone else, but I was wrong.'

Now a roving ambassador for a mixture of corporate and charitable concerns, Pelé travels the world extolling the beauty of the game, shaking hands with people and generally being a thoroughly nice guy. He still expresses surprise that so many people want to meet him, which sums him up rather nicely.

This was a man so good at football that he could stop wars, and that's no exaggeration. His presence at an exhibition match in Lagos in 1967 forced the two warring factions in the Nigerian civil war to down tools in a 48-hour ceasefire agreed specifically so that everyone could watch the game. As good as Cristiano Ronaldo is, he's yet to have any impact in Afghanistan, isn't he?

Diego Maradona

If Pelé, with his sunny disposition and charm, represented all that was good about the game, then Maradona did his best to provide a counterbalance. Every bit as talented as the Brazilian, perhaps even more so depending on who you ask, his career was blighted by drug use, personal problems, outright cheating and one absolutely awesome airgun shoot-out with journalists.

Like Pelé, Maradona was the product of poverty, honing his skills in a shantytown on the outskirts of Buenos Aires. He began his career with Argentinos Juniors before moving to Boca Juniors in 1981. An astonishingly skilful player, he was absolutely tiny but was built like a breeze block. His low centre of balance made it difficult for anyone to knock him off the ball and his superhuman close control meant that he could zip through packed defences at waist level, moving the ball from left foot to right foot so quickly that no one could get near it.

He soon caught the attention of Barcelona, who brought him to Spain in a world record transfer deal, but Maradona found life hard in La Liga. He clashed with senior management, suffered illness and injury and eventually demanded a transfer. He moved to Napoli in 1984 and it was in Italy that he achieved his greatest success at club level, two Serie A titles, the equivalent of the Premier League or SPL, with a relatively unsuccessful, but passionately backed team.

Before that, however, he was responsible for one of the most infamous moments in World Cup history when he punched the ball past goalkeeper Peter Shilton in Argentina's 1986 clash with England. Despite the fact that every man, woman and child could see that it was handball, the officials missed it and the goal counted. England went out of the tournament and Maradona gleefully claimed that the goal was scored by 'the hand of God.' He's not been too popular in England since then, although he was practically deified in Scotland. Argentina went on to win the trophy, led to glory single-handedly, quite literally, by the amazing Maradona.

However, personal problems eventually caught up with him. His cocaine habit spiralled out of control and he was banned from football for 15 months in 1992. He returned to lead Argentina to the 1994 World Cup before failing a drugs test there and being sent home. Jaw-dropping weight gain soon followed, as did unwelcome paternity suits, more drugs and that famous shoot-out with a crew of journalists who had unwisely besieged him at his home. It's not fashionable to like Maradona if you're English, but how can you not appreciate that kind of behaviour, eh?

George Best

For all that has ever been written about him, it was George Best himself who most aptly summed up his own career. 'If I'd have been born ugly,' he said, 'you'd never have heard of Pelé.' He was absolutely right. Gifted with extraordinary talent and the determination to hone it, he was cursed with pop star good looks and a fondness for drink that would eventually destroy him.

Born in Belfast, Best was an outstanding talent for his local boys' team, but was acutely aware that his left foot was weaker than his right. To rectify this, he trained for hours on his own before eventually playing in one match with a boot on his left foot and a plimsoll on his right. He scored six goals on what was no longer his weaker foot and it wasn't long before he'd attracted the attention of Manchester United.

He was signed by Sir Matt Busby and made his debut in 1963, quickly winning over the fans with his genius. An integral part of the first post-Munich United team to win the title, he came to prominence with two goals away at Benfica in the European Cup, a performance that earned him the nickname 'O Quinto Beatle', the fifth Beatle.

And here's where the trouble began. A mixture of home-sickness and shyness led to Best's over-reliance on the bottle, a problem exacerbated by his sudden fame and near-constant appearances in some of the 1960s' most trendy nightspots. Soon he was appearing at the front of the papers as regularly as he was at the back, mainly because of the string of beautiful women that he appeared with.

He won the European Cup with United in 1968, but left the club in acrimonious circumstances in 1974, aged just 27. It was the beginning of the end of his career. His next club was Dunstable Town, a non-league side managed by his youth team friend Barry Fry. From there he went on a whistle-stop tour of small-time teams before a brief renaissance at Fulham in between spells in the North American Soccer League.

In the mid 80s, Best's alcoholism really took over. He spent Christmas 1984 in prison after a drink-driving offence and made one horrific appearance on a UK chat show while absolutely bladdered. He gave up the bottle and was given a liver transplant in 2002, and for a while he seemed to be on the mend. Unfortunately, his sobriety was relatively brief and he eventually died in 2005.

Paul Gascoigne

Paul Gascoigne should perhaps have been the greatest player of his generation, but a series of self-inflicted injuries, his mental instability and the onset of alcoholism prevented him from ever reaching his full potential.

He came to prominence during the 1990 World Cup in Italy, where his exceptional set-pieces and surging runs made him a firm favourite with England fans, but the enduring image of the young Geordie was not a happy one. Booked earlier in the tournament, Gascoigne knew that another yellow card in the semi-finals against Germany would mean that he would be suspended for the World Cup Final, should England progress. But Gascoigne was a passionate, committed player and the concept of pulling out of tackles to preserve himself was alien to him. Inevitably, he was booked and he promptly burst into tears. This sudden display of weakness and vulnerability shocked the nation. Men simply didn't cry in 1990, at least not in the open where people could see. The public were captivated and Gascoigne's fate was sealed.

England lost on penalties, but when Gascoigne returned he was a national hero. A sudden rise to superstardom is difficult for most people, for someone as daft as him it was a disaster waiting to happen. But as well as his legendary streak of mischief, he was beset by mental problems ranging from the trauma of seeing his friend killed as a child, to homesickness, bipolar disorder, bulimia and obsessive compulsive disorder. Unsurprisingly, he began to drink more than was good for him.

The first and most promising stage of his career ended at the 1991 FA Cup Final when he launched himself at Nottingham Forest's Gary Charles and ruptured the cruciate ligaments in his own knee, a career-threatening injury for which he could only blame himself. He eventually recovered to complete a transfer to Lazio in Italy, but he was never quite the same player again.

While Gascoigne no longer had the dramatic acceleration of old, he was still a great player. As well as three mixed years in Serie A, the second stage of his career saw him win trophies and personal honours galore in Scotland with Rangers, as well as spells with Middlesbrough and Everton. His finest hour came when he scored a magical goal for England against Scotland in the 1996 European Championships.

But Gascoigne's career eventually ebbed away, his legacy tarnished by a series of lurid tabloid headlines. A wonderfully gifted player, affable and generous to a fault, he remains the 'don't end up like him' horror story for a younger generation of footballers.

Bobby Moore

Tall, blonde and good-looking, Bobby Moore was as close to a classic comic book character as a footballer has ever been. He was everything you could want in a defender, everything a manager needs in a captain and a perfect role model for fans. He captained West Ham United, his local side, to FA Cup glory, but is most famous for lifting the World Cup in 1966 for England.

Interestingly, Moore was never considered to be an innately world class footballer. There were better headers of the ball and he wasn't very quick, but it didn't matter. No one could time a tackle quite like him because he had such an uncanny ability to read the game.

'There should be a law against him,' said Scottish manager Jock Stein. 'Bobby knows what is going to happen 20 minutes before anyone else.'

Pelé rated him as one of the best defenders he'd ever played against, as well as the fairest and if you ask any West Ham fans about him, they'll tell you that he never left the pitch with dirty shorts. He didn't need to launch into last-ditch tackles, because he always snuffed out threats before they became a danger.

That isn't to say that he couldn't get physical when he needed to. Team-mate Geoff Hurst knew that. 'Someone would come and kick a lump out of him and he'd play as though he hadn't noticed,' said Hurst. 'But 10 minutes later, whoof! He had a great golden boy image, Moore. But he was hard.'

But while Moore's playing career was glorious, his life after retirement was tragic. His business dealings cost him the bulk of his career earnings, sometimes through poor judgement, but sometimes through appalling luck, like his decision to relocate his leather goods factory to northern Cyprus just weeks before Turkey invaded.

He tried his hand at football management with Oxford City and Southend United, but with little success and in the late 80s he was reduced to writing for the downmarket tabloid, the *Sunday Sport*. An improvement of sorts arrived in 1991 when he began a career as a co-commentator for a London radio station, but just as he began to enjoy life again he was diagnosed with bowel cancer. Moore had already fought testicular cancer in 1962, but this was to be too much for him. He died in 1993 at the age of just 51.

Sir Stanley Matthews

Stanley Matthews began his professional football career in 1932 and retired from the English game in 1965 at the age of 50. If that was all that could be said about the man it would still be an extraordinary story, but Matthews wasn't blessed just with longevity. He was the wizard of dribble, a creative force without comparison and a man who Pelé himself claimed 'taught us the way football should be played.'

He signed for Stoke in 1930 as a 15 year old and played for them until 1947 when he moved to Blackpool after a dispute with the club's management.

'You're 32,' said Blackpool's manager Joe Smith when his

new signing arrived. 'Do you think you can make it for another couple of years?'

Matthews managed another 14 years before then returning to Stoke for four more. He even ended up in Malta as player-manager of Hibernians in 1970, pulling on a shirt for the final time at the age of 55.

But it is the 1953 FA Cup Final for which Matthews is most famous. With Blackpool trailing Bolton Wanderers 1-3 in the second half, he inspired them to a memorable 4-3 comeback and the game has become forever known as 'The Matthews Final', something which could be considered a little harsh on Stan Mortensen, who actually scored a hat-trick that day.

But it was Matthews' wing-play that created the goals, as it always tended to be so for every team he played for. Tommy Lawton, a team-mate of his for England once said, 'He used to put the ball on my centre-parting. They don't do that anymore.'

'Stan was unique,' said another international colleague, Joe Mercer. 'He never went for 50-50 balls, didn't score many goals and was not good in the air. But on his day he was unplayable. He beat fellows so easily, with such pace and balance, often taking on four or five (players) at a time.'

Matthews died in 2000 at the age of 85 and his funeral was attended by the great and the good of world football. The wing wizard's ashes were buried under the centre spot at Stoke City's new ground, the Britannia Stadium. Ironic really, it's probably the most central position he's ever occupied.

The ground

Things not to do

When you go to a real, live football match for the first time, you have to be wary. Like any other social pursuit there is a long-established code of conduct. Most of the people around you will have been going for many years, often sat in exactly the same place, season in, season out. Sitting down next to them and shouting your mouth off is a quick and easy ride to instant unpopularity. Here's a few things you shouldn't do.

Location

You would think it would be an obvious one, but don't sit in the end allocated to the opposition and then start cheering for your own team. There is a reason that football supporters are segregated and you don't want to find it out the hard way. The vast majority of fans are fine, upstanding, good-natured people, but if their team goes one-nil down and you jump up and down in celebration, they'll pull your arm off and beat you to death with the wet end.

Only the most disciplined of supporters can possibly hope to survive for 90 minutes in enemy territory without giving themselves away. If you really are going to do it then sit on your hands, bite the insides of your cheeks and, if your team goes one-nil down, you make damn sure you stand up and cheer. They are always watching.

Colours

Be a little bit careful about wearing team colours at an away match. It's not the 1980s and the level of violence on the streets outside football stadiums has dropped significantly, but not completely. Most sensible travelling fans, if going to a match on their own, will keep their replica shirt covered up and their scarf in their pocket until they reach the sanctuary of the away end. Cover up as you leave as well. The last thing you want to do is wander into a fish and chip shop after the game and find yourself outnumbered 20-1 by some robust gentlemen who have a rather different view of that last-minute penalty decision. Denying your footballing faith for a short time isn't that bad and the players aren't going to find out that you did it. It's just simple self-preservation and there's nothing wrong with that.

Food

For the love of God, don't eat the food inside a football stadium. This advice comes in capital letters and in bold font if you're outside the Premier League, and in 12ft high neon if you're in a non-league ground. Football food is ludicrously over-priced and rarely made with the kind of tender care and watchfulness that your body will thank you for afterwards. Take it from someone who has eaten out at some of League One's most insalubrious venues; the journey home will be a long one if your stomach is bubbling and fizzing like a witch's cauldron. You're a lot better off finding a local takeaway or greasy spoon instead, or even just, you know, eating before you leave the house. Besides, getting served generally takes at least five to ten minutes longer than the half-time break, so if you want to get your food and eat it before play restarts, you have to leave your seat in the 35th minute and, if you're skipping the football to fill yourself up on toxic meat by-products, you have to question why you came along in the first place.

Booing your own players

Jeering your own players is not something to be entered into lightly and it is the kind of thing that can cause moments of distinct unpleasantness. There are a great many football fans who believe that their players should be supported whole-heartedly and unflinchingly throughout the game and they will be only too quick to let you know what they think of 'splitters' or 'fairweather fans'. You have to remember that the people around you have been there for some time and they may have different interpretations of what constitutes a good shift in their shirt. Peter Crouch, on arriving at Liverpool in 2005, went 19 games without scoring and the Anfield regulars were forced to defend him against the taunts from the daytrippers who couldn't see how hard he was working. It wasn't a good time to be a daytripper, or a 'wool' as they call them up there.

That said, there are moments when the only thing you can do is to boo: England's pitiful first-half 'efforts' against Andorra in 2007 being a case in point. Just be very careful and think before you make that round shape with your lips. Not many players improve when they hear their own fans turning against them.

Starting songs

No one is entirely sure how football songs start, but one thing is certain: it's not through the efforts of one lone newcomer stood on his own, waving his arms in the air and getting the words wrong. Join in, for sure, but don't try and get the hearts of an entire football stadium beating to your rhythm on your first trip to the ground.

Standing

Everyone who's ever been to a football match knows that standing is much more fun than sitting. You can't sing properly down there and if you're any taller than 5ft 8in you get your knees caught on the back of the seat in front of you. It's rubbish. However, since the Taylor Report and the introduction of all-seater stadiums, it is the law and it's been the law for long enough for everyone to stop getting so upset about it.

The vast majority of football fans hate being told to sit down, but then the vast majority of football fans are not old-age pensioners or children forced to spend an afternoon staring helplessly at someone else's back. Every time you stand up, the person behind you has to stand up and so on and so forth until a little old man with knees as brittle as a cheese cracker loses his view of the goal of the season and is forced to wonder why he spent most of his pension on not being able to see the football. Standing is acceptable if you're lucky enough to have seats right at the back of the stand where you can't obscure anyone's vision.

There are admirable campaigns to bring back standing, and getting involved with one of them is far more constructive than being pig-headed and ruining someone's day.

The pub

Things to say

If you can't get a ticket for the big game, there's always the option of going to the pub. It'll have a big screen, comfy seats and all the liquid refreshment required to make even the dullest game look entertaining. Unless of course it's Bolton Wanderers. Nobody has invented a drink *that* good.

The pub experience is a little different from the live game as, although both venues are full of people who have squandered far too much time and money within its boundaries, the average drinker is liable to be less passionate and more amenable to a passing chat, especially if it isn't his team playing.

If you're in the pub with friends then what follows is of no consequence, but if you're with new people or even dropping into conversation with a complete stranger, you'll only have a short period of time to prove that you know what you're talking about. Get something wrong in the first five minutes of a chat and your point of view will be scorned and then forever ignored. You'll probably have to find a new pub.

So with that in mind, here's a big list of things to say that will have your audience nodding sagely and agreeing with you in no time.

Pre-game

'Look at the state of that pitch! How are [insert team here] going to perform on that?'

If you're trying to pass a football accurately then it's easier to do it on a surface like a billiard table than it is on a freshly ploughed field. Keep an eye out for the suspicious-looking patches of mud or sand as the TV cameras sweep around the stadium beforehand. Picking up on the terrain will make people think that you used to play and linking it to the tactics of a team will have them eating out of your hand.

DO Keep an eye out as the game progresses and warm to your theme by announcing, 'I told you. It's cutting up already.'

DO NOT Proclaim that the conditions will hurt a team that play long ball. Only the sophisticated teams will struggle.

'They should be playing [insert young star's name here]. If you're good enough, you're old enough.'

Ever since TV pundit Alan Hansen opined that Manchester United wouldn't win anything with kids (they won the double), football fans have darted in the opposite direction, demanding the inclusion of fresh-faced children who should really be doing their homework. Happily, a quick name check of the rising starlets in your ranks will pay instant dividends. Not only will you look like you know your own team, you'll look like you know your own youth team as well.

DO Make sure that the player in question is at least 17. Anything less and it's borderline child labour.

DO NOT Ever use this argument if you're talking about goalkeepers and be wary if the youngster is a defender. These positions are perceived to be the domain of grizzled veterans.

'This Spanish/Nigerian/Peruvian lad is good, but how's he going to cope with a wet Tuesday night in Bolton, eh?'
In the minds of football supporters, footballers from warmer climes are a kind of wimpish sub-species, who can be seen openly weeping when the temperature drops into single figures and appear to be allergic to mud. Alarmingly, this can often be the case and it's not exactly rare to see a foreign import banging in the goals in August and then vanishing when the clocks go back. Seasoned observers know that it's often hard to tell a genuinely great player from a flash in the pan.

DO Feel free to play with the structure and insert your own variables. Be careful though. 'Snowy Wednesday night on Teesside' works. 'Pleasant afternoon in Shropshire' does not.

DO NOT Be too quick to mock. A lot of African players began their careers at small European clubs. If he's just done three years in Norway, I reckon he'll be fine in Manchester.

Mid-game
'If in doubt, kick it out!'
Most goals stem from mistakes and if the defenders are carelessly knocking the ball to each other in their own penalty area or attempting to dribble through to the halfway line, you can usually expect something to go horribly wrong. A quick burst of this classic, uncompromising refrain will make you look alert to the situation as well as delivering the bonus of making you look authentic and old school. Defensive sophistication? That's not very English, is it?

DO Play with the verb. Kick can just as easily be 'put', 'punt', 'thump', or 'whack'. How about 'hoof'? Everyone loves a hoof! Always be ready to add your own artistic flourish.

DO NOT Say this immediately after ranting about the technical shortcomings of the English game.

'It's got nil-nil written all over it.'

There are some games that you just know are going to be awful. If two teams are getting closer to knocking out the floodlights than they are to scoring a goal, or if the referee is blowing his whistle every time a player coughs out of turn, you can be fairly sure you've wasted an evening watching an awful game. The first person brave enough to say it out loud gets to feel like the pub's resident soothsayer.

DO Always laugh heartily if you are almost instantly proved wrong. You might not have the ability to predict goalless draws, but apparently you have the power to prevent them.

DO NOT Walk into the pub ten minutes after kick-off and drop this little nugget in without looking at the scoreboard first.

'He's going to talk his way into the book if he's not careful.'

Referees, as you now know, have the ability to caution players who constantly argue with their decisions, and proper football fans despise dissent, especially if it involves members of their team getting themselves booked unnecessarily. It's rather counter-productive to run after the referee calling him names if he then gets his own back by pulling out a second yellow card for the next mistimed tackle.

DO Shake your head as you say it. It will make you look like a disappointed guardian of all that is gallant in the game.

DO NOT Say this if the player talking to the referee is the captain. They're not actually supposed to vehemently dispute things, but they get some leeway and can 'discuss' decisions.

After an appeal for a penalty

'I've seen 'em given.'

The quintessential go-to soundbite for the completely confused, this one will really come in handy. If the ball is cannoned into a defender's hand and you're not sure if he had time to move out of the way, then you've seen 'em given. If the tackle seemed to impact on the ball first, but took a lot of the man, and you're not sure if that's good or bad, then you've seen 'em given. Innocuous-looking push or shirt-tug in the penalty area? You're getting the hang of it!

DO Precede the statement by sucking the air through your teeth like a mechanic trying to get away with an unusually high quote. It sounds better.

DO NOT Say this if the defender has leapt in with his studs at throat level, causing a five-minute stoppage while they mop the blood off the penalty spot. Unless you're being ironic.

'What's he doing? You can't make a substitution before a set-piece!'

The introduction of a new player can cause confusion and the last place you want to be confused is in your own area guarding a set-piece. When a team is defending corners or free-kicks, they will all have had time to get used to their instructions; a new man might bumble on to the pitch, stand in the wrong place and ruin it for everyone. Most managers like to make sure that a substitute's first contribution isn't to apologise to his team-mates for not marking that striker.

DO Add enough passion to your voice to suggest that the

manager's decision is as ludicrous as putting ice cream on toast. Who would do such a thing?

DO NOT Allow the fact that the set-piece will almost certainly be competently defended to put you off. If danger passes, just shake your head, exhale and comment on the manager's good fortune.

After a goal

'And that's why you have men on both posts.'

This little gem is dual purpose. You can say it in dismay if a corner leads to the opposition scoring an entirely preventable goal, or you can say it with a big grin on your face when your defender successfully heads a ball off the line at a set-piece. Men are usually positioned on the posts to give the goalkeeper the freedom to come out and claim crosses, or to act as an insurance policy against nasty deflections. Pointing this out will make you look like someone who knows their tactics.

DO Be careful who you say this to. Announcing it mockingly, or in the form of a song, to a supporter of the side who have just conceded is silly. People can be touchy.

DO NOT Let the fact that the manager probably played 20 years of professional football before embarking on a successful coaching career get in your way. He needs telling.

'Right before half-time. That's the best time to score.'

For some reason, there seems to be a tendency for a goal before half-time to completely turn a game on its head. More than likely, it's because the team who scored go down the tunnel at the break with a spring in their step and the opposition have to sit there being shouted at for switching off at such an important time. Whatever the reason, it's a curious phenomenon and well worth pointing out.

DO Make sure that you pick your moments. Scoring an equaliser, or a goal that turns a 0-2 into 1-2, is relevant. Picking up a consolation strike to make it 1-4 probably isn't.

DO NOT Worry if no discernible effect is evident after the break. Memories are short in pubs and the second half may as well be next week to your fellow converser.

After a red card

'It's harder to play against ten men than eleven.'

This is the kind of glorious nonsense upon which the entire edifice of football rests. Of course it shouldn't be harder to play against fewer players, but the numerically weaker side will instantly change their tactics, drop deep and try to hold out for a draw. So you can actually get away with voicing such lunacy because everyone will nod and agree and you'll look like you've been watching for years. Bonkers.

DO Say this with a faraway look in your eyes; a thousand-yard stare that hints of a deep wound from the past. No one will question you.

DO NOT Think that it is therefore twice as hard to play against nine men. It doesn't work like that.

Picking teams

So, you know the rules, you know the tactics, you know the history and the traditions. But do you know who you support? In most instances, football supporters don't choose their team, their team chooses them. The decision is made unwittingly at primary school, or passed down to them by a relative. In your case, as a new arrival to the game, it may be a little different. But don't worry, you'll make the right decision.

The chances are that you already know who you should be following. It might be the local team whose reports have caught your eye in the paper, or whose cup run stole your attention a few years ago. It might be the team that someone in your family or your partner supports. It might just be that you tuned in and watched the live game a few weeks ago and fell in love with one of the teams on display.

Beware. Football fans get very aggressive about authenticity. If you've got an Essex accent, you can't just walk into a United pub in the centre of Manchester and expect to be welcomed with open arms. It doesn't matter how much merchandise you buy, the locals may still regard you as a 'daytripper'. You should also be aware of the rivalries between clubs that intensify their meetings. If you live in Sunderland, is it really wise to adopt Newcastle? And if all of your friends support Liverpool, then going to Goodison Park to watch Everton might get a bit lonely. Make sure you do your research! To avoid such pitfalls, it's worth bearing in mind the following points.

Glory

The easy option is simply to pick the most successful team in the country and just follow them. After all, they've got the best players and they win most of the time. What's not to like? This is a perfectly understandable, but ultimately flawed view. Lending your weight to the champions for no other reason than to bask in their reflected glory is like buying shares in a company just after they announce record profits. You can take no satisfaction in having spotted a bargain and the only way is down. Scattered about the world are hordes of Blackburn Rovers fans who leapt onto the mid-90s bandwagon when they won the league title under Kenny Dalglish and have been doomed thereafter to follow the gallant, but hopeless efforts of a small, unfashionable team in the north-west of England. Don't let yourself suffer their awful fate. For those first few months, everything must have been wonderful and yet now it all seems so futile.

You are only ever allowed to change your team if you follow a big side on TV and then find yourself 're-educated' by a trip to your local club, although this only works if you trade down and it only works once. People who switch teams like they switch coffee brands are ostracised from society, and rightly so. What do you believe in if you don't believe in your football team? What kind of person deserts their team in the darkest hour? Not the kind of person I want in my front room.

Geography

There is little point in choosing to support a team who play in a stadium miles away from your house. Whether they are European regulars or low league scrappers, you won't be going to see them very often if it involves a 300-mile round trip. Watching football on the television is a wonderful thing, but going to see games in the flesh is far superior. You get the noise, the smells, the feeling that you're part of something special. It's far nicer just to be able to jump on the bus and reach the stadium than it is to spend a significant proportion of your life on Britain's motorways.

Don't rule out the team nearest to you, no matter how unglamorous they seem. Supporting a small local team gives you a strange feeling of ownership, primarily because in a funny kind of way you actually do own the club. It is your ticket money, not TV subscriptions from Asia and not the sale of duvet sets from the megastores, that keeps the team afloat. It is your voice that the players hear when they take to the pitch, sometimes all too clearly if the attendance is really small. At the really low levels, the players thank you personally if you congratulate them on a good tackle.

It also means that the rewards for success are all the greater because there are fewer people with whom to share the rare moments of glory. You put up with the dross for years and then suddenly you get an unbelievable result in the cup and your head explodes. Ask Portsmouth supporters how it felt to win the FA Cup in 2008. Ask Carlisle fans what it meant to return from the bowels of non-league in 2005. It's all a bit more intense when it really is 'your' team.

Family

There's nothing wrong with following a good example and if

someone in your family introduced you to football with stories of days at the old Stretford End or standing on the Kop at Anfield, then most fans will accept you supporting one of the big teams, no matter where you live. A love of football is something passed down through the generations, though you might want to be quick on the draw with your heritage when meeting new people. In football you are guilty of glory-hunting until proven innocent and the idea of a Cornish Liverpool fan is still a bit of a leap into the unknown for some older fans.

Being different

Yes, Accrington Stanley have got a very funny name and it certainly is something of a talking point in the pub to introduce yourself as one of their supporters, but seriously? How long is it going to take for that to get boring if you actually live in Kent and you've got no idea who's in the first team?

Ignoring all advice

Of course, you could read all of this and think me a crushing bore for daring to give any guidelines as to who an individual should and should not support. You'd be quite right as well. You have the freedom to support anyone you like and you certainly don't need my permission to inexplicably throw your heart and soul into a team of ready-made superstars and heroes. These days, the saturation coverage of football means that you can catch the majority of the big teams on television every week. But just remember that, when it comes to fiery debates in the pub on a Friday night, if your accent doesn't fit, you may find yourself having to defend your own honour as well as the honour of the team you have chosen.

Glossary

Arsenal Football team based in North London. One of the biggest clubs in England known for their fancy, sophisticated style these days, but formerly the home of some very, very boring football indeed.

Assistant referees Those chaps running up and down the sidelines with flags in their hands. Formerly known as 'linesmen' or 'linoes', they assist the referee with his decisions, primarily making calls on throw-ins, corners and offsides.

Association Football The official name of the sport. The name 'soccer' comes from the abbreviation ASSOC.

Attacker One of a group of players whose main aim is to score goals.

Back pass The goalkeeper cannot pick the ball up if it has been passed back to him by the feet of a defender. If the ball is headed back, it's absolutely fine, but handling the ball after it has been kicked there will result in an indirect free-kick.

Baddiel and Skinner Comedians behind the cult classic *Fantasy Football* show. Baddiel and Skinner also wrote the anthemic song 'Three Lions' for Euro96, the tournament which confirmed English football's return to the mainstream.

Bench Where the manager and the substitutes sit on the sidelines. To be 'left on the bench' is to be made a substitute.

Brazil The 1970 Brazil team is regarded as the finest footballing side of all time. If a team is playing gorgeous football, you may hear the song 'It's Just Like Watching Brazil', which might be accurate if you're watching Arsenal or Manchester United, but is a ludicrous thing for, say, a Colchester United fan to chant.

Bullard, Jimmy Fluffy-haired, perma-grinning midfielder for a host of unfashionable clubs in the 21st century. A cult hero with fans simply because he is one of the few professional footballers who actually looks like he's having fun.

Buying a throw-in/corner Deliberately kicking the ball at the opposition in the hope that it rebounds off and over the touchline, winning a set-piece. Very sneaky, but difficult to execute.

Cantona, Eric Wonderfully talented Manchester United striker. Bit moody though. He once karate-kicked a spectator who shouted something nasty at him.

Centre-back Alternative name for the defenders who ... erm ... defend in the centre of the pitch.

Corner If the defending team touches the ball last and the ball goes behind the goal-line, a corner is awarded. The ball is kicked back into play by the attacking team.

Cross To kick the ball from the flanks into the penalty area of the goal, in the hope that an attacker, or indeed anyone, will score a goal. Lots of goals come from crosses.

Defender One of a group of footballers whose main aim is to stop the other team scoring.

Dribbling Running along with the ball at your feet.

Dropping deep Footballers gravitating towards their own goal in an effort to either shake off markers or help out their defence.

European Championships An international tournament held every four years.

European Cup The former name of the Champions League.

FA Cup The oldest football tournament in the world, famous for the occasional giant-killing and mostly boring finals.

Fédération Internationale de Football Association (FIFA) The world's governing body of football.

Football Fables Timeless and exquisitely put-together anthology of stories from some of the most interesting characters in the game. A must-read for any new football fans, it was published by A&C Black in 2008 and remains one of the finest books of its kind. That's what my mum said, anyway.

Football firms Gangs of football hooligans who, like Bananarama, were all over the newspapers in the 1980s, but don't get spotted so often now.

Formation A series of numbers denoting the set-up of a football team (4-4-2, 4-3-3 etc.)

Foul An offence against the rules. Like kicking someone or handling the ball.

Fourth official Another referee's assistant, but one with no direct power over the game. The fourth official watches from the sidelines, organises substitutions, recommends periods of added time and tries to stop opposing managers scrapping with each other.

Free-kick Fouls result in free-kicks to the other team. These free-kicks can be direct or indirect depending on the offence.

Full-back A defender who defends a specific side of the pitch.

Usually named by their location (left-back or right-back), this is a generic term for both positions.

Gazza's tears The sobbing of Paul Gascoigne in the 1990 World Cup that captivated a nation. Generally thought to be one of the factors that made football popular again after the nadir of the 1980s.

Goal 1. The large net held together by white posts at either end of the pitch. Did you really need to look this up?

2. The name given to the moment that the entire ball crosses the line of the goal, inside those posts. So, to score a goal, you have to kick the ball in the goal. Then it is a goal. Ah, yes. That is a little confusing.

Goalkeeper Man in gloves who stands in the goal. He can use his hands; no one else can.

Goal-kick If the ball is kicked behind the goal by a member of the attacking team, play restarts with a kick by the goalkeeper or one of his team-mates from the edge of the six-yard box.

Half-time The break in-between the first half and the second half.

Handball Only the goalkeeper can touch the ball with his hand, and that's only inside the confines of his own area. For everyone else it's a foul.

Hand of God The description given to Diego Maradona's infamous handball goal of 1986 which knocked England out of the World Cup. Twenty-four years on and I'm still bitter about that. As is Peter Shilton actually.

Header Using your head to make contact with the football.

Hornby, Nick Author of the novel *Fever Pitch*, one of the first football books to be acclaimed by anyone other than sports journalists, primarily because it was written from a middle-class viewpoint and hinted that football might be rather more than just a thug's game. Occasionally blamed for the rise of the bourgeois fan, it is still well worth a read.

Injury time The period of time added on to the end of a game at the referee's discretion to compensate for time lost to injuries or other stoppages in play.

International language of football The phrase used to describe the phenomenon of long conversations that rely less on an understanding of each other's dialect and more on the ability to name players from each other's' nation.

Keane, Roy Terrifying Irish footballer and football manager. Keane played for Manchester United between 1993 and 2005 and picked up a truly awe-inspiring 11 red cards in the process.

Keegan, Kevin Much-loved football manager known for his boundless enthusiasm and devotion to the attacking game.

Kick-off The start of the game, held in the centre-circle.

Kilcline, Brian Terrifying 1980s centre-back who looked like a Hell's Angel.

Linesman/Lino *See* Assistant referee.

Manager The man who picks the team and the tactics.

Man-to-man marking Standing very close to an opponent to discourage his team-mates from passing to him and to make sure that, if they do, he can be stopped quickly.

Match of the Day Legendary Saturday night highlights show. One presenter, two pundits and a whole lot of football.

Midfielder One of a group of footballers whose main aim is to pass the ball or tackle to win it back.

Obstruction Standing in front of an opponent to prevent him reaching the ball. Punishable with an indirect free-kick.

Offside If an attacker is nearer to the goal than the second from last defender (usually including the goalkeeper) then he is offside and a free-kick is awarded when the referee judges him to be interfering with play.

Offside trap When a defence pushes up as one unit, leaving their opponents nearer to the goal than themselves, thus rendering them offside.

Olsen, Egil Norwegian football manager. Famous for boring but effective football.

O'Neill, Martin Northern Irish football manager known for inspiring his teams to play above their natural level.

Open play The free-flowing part of the game. Anything that isn't a throw-in, free-kick, penalty or corner really.

Own-goal Accidentally scoring in your own goal results in a goal for the other team. It's best avoided.

Pass The act of kicking the ball to one of your team-mates.

Penalty A foul inside the penalty area is rewarded with a penalty kick, also known as a spot kick. These are very difficult to miss, unless you happen to be English, in which case it's second nature.

Penalty area/box The big white box surrounding the goal. Fouls in here will be punished severely. *See* Penalty.

Pitch invasion The criminal offence of a spectator or spectators running on to the pitch. Used to involve hundreds of people, now more likely to be a fat bloke with his willy out or a lone drunk being chased by stewards.

Play-offs Extraordinarily exciting end-of-season mini-tournament held to determine the winners of the extra promotion place. Finals are held at Wembley.

Possession Passing the ball round the team is a way of keeping the ball in possession. Thumping it artlessly down the pitch is a good way to lose possession.

Pushing up Footballers gravitating towards their opponent's goal in an effort to either help out the attack or to catch their opponents offside. *See* Offside.

Red card If a referee flashes one of these at an offending player then it's the end of his game. Red-carded players are sent off, banished from the football match.

Referee The poor man whose job it is to maintain order during the football match. *See also* Assistant Referee.

Relegation dogfight A league fixture between struggling football clubs, usually at the end of the season. Teams in danger of relegation tend to dispense with pleasantries and scrap for survival, hence the feral connotations of the phrase.

Route one A tactic designed to get the ball from one end of the pitch to the other as quickly as possible, usually by punting it hard into the air. Very boring to watch, but can be effective.

Russian Linesman Genuine hero who awarded England a dubious goal in their 4-2 victory over Germany. He's from Azerbaijan really, though.

Save The act of a goalkeeper using a part of his body, any part, to prevent the ball going into the goal.

Set-pieces Corners, free-kicks even throw-ins. A generic term for moments in the game that are not open. *See* Open play.

Shot Kicking the ball at the goal in the hope of scoring a goal. Come on! You knew that already!

Six-pointer A crunch match between two similarly placed teams, usually at the end of the season. At this stage of the campaign, not only are teams desperate to win games for three points, but they are also hoping that their rivals will lose and drop three points. When they go head-to-head, they have a chance to ensure both objectives are met with one game, hence the 'six-point' reference. You don't actually get six points though. That would be silly.

Six-yard box The smaller box inside the penalty area. Goal-kicks are taken from the edge of this.

Striker *See* Attacker.

Southend United Plucky lower-league team with a habit of humiliating Premier League sides in the cup competitions. A fine body of men.

Substitute A spare player, used as a replacement for an injured, tired, useless or otherwise unwanted team-mate.

Tackle Dispossession of an opponent by kicking or blocking the ball as they come near.

Taylor Report The epoch-shaking government report about the Hillsborough disaster that called for the abolition of fencing fans in and the introduction of all-seater stadia.

Throw-in The act of restarting the football match when the ball has passed over the touchlines at the sides of the pitch.

Wall The human wall of defenders used to block free-kicks.

Wembley Stadium The home of English football, a gigantic new stadium in North London built to replace the old Wembley Stadium.

Winger A midfielder who plays on a specific side of the pitch. Usually named by their location (left-winger or right-winger), this is a generic term for both the left and right positions.

World Cup The 32-team tournament that brings together the finest nations in the world for a month-long festival of football, usually resulting in England's elimination on penalties.

Vidiprinter Archaic device used to deliver football scorelines from across the country. The now-defunct Saturday afternoon sports show *Grandstand* would 'go to the vidiprinter' and switch to a constantly updating word processor page with newly arriving scorelines making a reassuring 'biddybiddybiddybiddyphut' noise as they were typed out on the screen. Groundbreaking for its time, I assure you.

Yellow card A warning shot across the bow of an offending player. A yellow card is the referee saying, 'That's almost it for you, matey. One more foul and I'm sending you off.' Two yellows, you see, make a red. *See also* Red card.

Zonal marking Marking a specific space on the pitch, rather than a player.

Index